# BIOMEDICAL-ETHICAL ISSUES
A Digest of Law and Policy Development

93870

Printed in the United States of America by
Vail-Ballou Press, Inc., Binghamton, N.Y.

Library of Congress catalogue card number: 82–13394
International standard book number: 0–300–02974–8

10   9   8   7   6   5   4   3   2   1

# CONTENTS

# INTRODUCTION

The moral issues raised by recent developments in biomedical science and health care have caused a great deal of activity in the realm of public policy. Courts have made precedent-setting decisions; the Congress has written laws or established agencies that write guidelines with the force of law; recent presidents have appointed commissions that make recommendations, many of which become law; state legislatures have promulgated their own laws. To influence the development of law and public opinion, churches and other religious bodies have issued policy statements; professional organizations, such as the American Medical Association, have studied and announced positions; national and international organizations, such as the United Nations, have also issued declarations.

This digest presents a brief summary of recent public policy developments--those that carry the force of law as well as those that seek to influence the development of law. For the most part, excerpts from the original documents are provided. The topics are limited to five because this digest is intended to be a supplemental resource to a primary text for class use and study groups, Health and Human Values: A Guide to Making Your Own Decisions, by Frank Harron, John Burnside, M.D., and Tom Beauchamp (New Haven and London:Yale University Press, 1983), which explores more and broader bioethical issues.

The purposes for which this digest is intended to serve are:

1. to present a brief summary, using excerpts from primary sources, of recent public policy developments;

2. to juxtapose competing positions advocated within a pluralistic society;

3. to inform citizens of the current status of public policy in these five areas (However, changes happen quickly and the reader is advised to seek the most recent information on his or her own.);

4.  to demonstrate areas in which current public policy is var-
    ied, in some cases contradictory, in different states; and

5.  to provide a convenient resource for educators, attorneys,
    legislators, citizen-activists, and others.

     Several persons are responsible for the compilation of this
digest.  Much of the original accumulation of documents was done
by Nadya Shmavonian.  George Annas, J.D., M.P.H., Associate Professor of Law and Medicine at the School of Medicine of Boston
University, revised Ms. Shmavonian's work and put the manuscript
into its next-to-last draft.  Judith Areen, J.D., Professor of
Law at the Georgetown School of Law, read the manuscript and made
suggestions, many of which were incorporated into the manuscript.
Mrs. Edna Boulden, Miss Adaline Wentz, and Mr. Kirk Hoffmeier
typed the manuscript.  To these persons, I express my thanks.

                                        Frank M. Harron
                                        September 1982

# I. ABORTION AND PRENATAL PROCEDURES


## A. Permitting Abortions


### 1. The Abortion Decisions


#### a. *Roe v. Wade*, 410 U.S. 113 (1973)

Mr. Justice Blackmun delivered the opinion of the Court.

This Texas federal appeal and its Georgia companion, Doe v Bolton, 410 US 179, 35 L Ed 2d 201, 93 S Ct 789, present constitutional challenges to state criminal abortion legislation. The Texas statutes under attack here are typical of those that have been in effect in many States for approximately a century. The Georgia statutes, in contrast, have a modern cast and are a legislative product that, to an extent at least, obviously reflects the influences of recent attitudinal change, of advancing medical knowledge and techniques, and of new thinking about an old issue.

We forthwith acknowledge our awareness of the sensitive and emotional nature of the abortion controversy, of the vigorous opposing views, even among physicians, and of the deep and seemingly absolute convictions that the subject inspires. One's philosophy, one's experiences, one's exposure to the raw edges of human existence, one's religious training, one's attitudes toward life and family and their values, and the moral standards one establishes and seeks to observe, are all likely to influence and to color one's thinking and conclusions about abortion.

In addition, population growth, pollution, poverty, and racial overtones tend to complicate and not to simplify the problem.

Our task, of course, is to resolve the issue by constitutional measurement, free of emotion and of predilection. We seek earnestly to do this, and, because we do, we inquired into, and in this opinion place some emphasis upon, medical and medical-legal history and what that history reveals about man's attitudes toward the abortion procedure over the cen-

1

turies.  We bear in mind, too, Mr. Justice Holmes' admonition in
his now-vindicated dissent in Lochner v New York, 198 US 45, 76,
49 L Ed 937, 25 S Ct 539 (1905):

> "[The Constitution] is made for people of fundamentally dif-
> fering views, and the accident of our finding certain opin-
> ions natural and familiar or novel and even shocking ought
> not to conclude our judgment upon the question whether stat-
> utes embodying them conflict with the Constitution of the
> United States."

The Texas statutes that concern us here are Arts. 1191-1194
and 1196 of the State's Penal Code.  These make it a crime to
"procure an abortion," as therein defined, or to attempt one,
except with respect to "an abortion procured or attempted by
medical advice for the purpose of saving the life of the
mother."  Similar statutes are in existence in a majority of the
States.

Jane Roe, a single woman who was residing in Dallas County,
Texas, instituted this federal action in  March 1970 against the
District Attorney of the county.  She sought a declaratory judgment that the Texas criminal abortion statutes were unconstitutional on their face, and an injunction restraining the defendant from enforcing the statutes.

Roe alleged that she was unmarried and pregnant; that she
wished to terminate her pregnancy by an abortion "performed by a
competent, licensed physician, under safe, clinical conditions";
that she was unable to get a "legal" abortion in Texas because
her life did not appear to be threatened by the continuation of
her pregnancy; and that she could not afford to travel to another jurisdiction in order to secure a legal abortion under
safe conditions.  She claimed that the Texas statutes were un-
constitutionally vague and that they abridged her right of personal privacy, protected by the First, Fourth, Fifth, Ninth, and
Fourteenth Amendments.  By an amendment to her complaint Roe
purported to sue "on behalf of herself and all other women" similarly situated.

James Hubert Hallford, a licensed physician, sought and was
granted leave to intervene in Roe's action.  In his complaint he
alleged that he had been arrested previously for violations of
the Texas abortion statutes and that two such prosecutions were
pending against him.  He described conditions of patients who
came to him seeking abortions, and he claimed that for many
cases he, as a physician, was unable to determine whether they
fell within or outside the exception recognized by Article 1196.
He alleged that, as a consequence, the statutes were vague and
uncertain, in violation of the Fourteenth Amendment, and that
they violated his own and his patients' rights to privacy in the
doctor-patient relationship and his own right to practice medicine, rights he claimed were guaranteed by the First, Fourth,
Fifth, Ninth, and Fourteenth Amendments.

The principle thrust of appellant's attack on the Texas statutes is that they improperly invade a right, said to be possessed by the pregnant woman, to choose to terminate her pregnancy. Appellant would discover this right in the concept of personal "liberty" embodied in the Fourteenth Amendment's Due Process Clause; or in personal, marital, familial, and sexual privacy said to be protected by the Bill of Rights or its penumbras. . . . Before addressing this claim, we feel it desirable briefly to survey, in several aspects, the history of abortion, for such insight as that history may afford us, and then to examine the state purposes and interests behind the criminal abortion laws.

It perhaps is not generally appreciated that the restrictive criminal abortion laws in effect in a majority of States today are of relatively recent vintage. Those laws, generally proscribing abortion or its attempt at any time during pregnancy except when necessary to preserve the pregnant woman's life, are not of ancient or even of common-law origin. Instead, they derive from statutory changes effected, for the most part, in the latter half of the 19th century.

1. *Ancient Attitudes.* These are not capable of precise determination. We are told that at the time of the Persian Empire abortifacients were known and that criminal abortions were severely punished. We are also told, however, that abortion was practiced in Greek times as well as in the Roman Era, and that "it was resorted to without scruple." The Ephesian, Soranos, often described as the greatest of the ancient gynecologists, appears to have been generally opposed to Rome's prevailing free-abortion practices. He found it necessary to think first of the life of the mother, and he resorted to abortion when, upon this standard, he felt the procedure advisable. Greek and Roman law afforded little protection to the unborn. If abortion was prosecuted in some places, it seems to have been based on a concept of a violation of the father's right to his offspring. Ancient relition did not bar abortion.

2. *The Hippocratic Oath.* The Oath varies somewhat according to the particular translation, but in any translation the content is clear: "I will give no deadly medicine to anyone if asked, nor suggest any such counsel; and in like manner I will not give to a woman a pessary to produce abortion." or "I will neither give a deadly drug to anybody if asked for it, nor will I make a suggestion to this effect. Similarly, I will not give to a woman an abortive remedy."

Although the Oath is not mentioned in any of the principal briefs in this case or in Doe v Bolton, 410 US 179, 35 L Ed 2d 201, 93 S Ct 739, it represents the apex of the development of strict ethical concepts in medicine, and its influence endures to this day. Why did not the authority of Hippocrates dissuade abortion practice in his time and that of Rome? The late Dr. Edelstein provides us with a theory: The Oath was not uncontested even in Hippocrates' day; only the Pythagorean school of philosophers frowned upon the related act of suicide. Most Greek thinkers, on the other hand, commended abortion, at least prior to viability. See Plato, Republic, V, 461; Aristotle, politics, VII, 1335b 25. For the Pythagoreans, however, it was a matter of dogma. For them the embryo was animate from the moment of conception, and abortion meant destruction of a living being. The abortion clause of the Oath, therefore, "echoes Pythagorean doctrines," and "[i]n no other stratum of Greek opinion were such views held or proposed in the same spirit of uncompromising austerity."

Edelstein then concludes that the Oath originated in a group representing only a small segment of Greek opinion and that it certainly was not accepted by all ancient physicians. He points out that medical writings down to Galen (A.D. 130-200) "give evidence of the violation of almost every one of its injunctions." But with the end of antiquity a decided change took place. Resistance against suicide and against abortion become common. The Oath came to be popular. The emerging teachings of Christianity were in agreement with the Phythagorean ethic. The Oath "became the nucleus of all medical ethics" and "was applauded as the embodiment of truth." Thus, suggests Dr. Edelstein, it is "a Pythagorean manifesto and not the expression of an absolute standard of medical conduct."

5. *The American law.* In this country, the law in effect in all but a few States until mid-19th century was the preexisting English common law. Connecticut, the first State to enact abortion legislation, adopted in 1821 that part of Lord Ellenborough's Act that related to a woman "quick with child." The death penalty was not imposed. Abortion before quickening was made a crime in that State only in 1860. In 1828, New York enacted legislation that, in two respects, was to serve as a model for early anti-abortion statutes. First, while barring destruction of an unquickened fetus as well as a quick fetus, it made the former only a misdemeanor, but the latter second-degree manslaughter. Second, it incorporated a concept of therapeutic abortion by providing that an abortion was excused if it "shall have been necessary to preserve the life of such mother, or shall have been advised by two physicians to be necessary for such purpose." By 1840, when Texas had received the common law, only eight American States had statutes dealing with abortion. It was not until after the War Between the States that legislation began generally to replace the common law. Most of these initial statutes dealt severely with abortion after quickening. Most punished attempts equally with completed abortions. While many statutes included the exception for an abortion thought by one or more physicians to be necessary to save the mother's life, that provision soon disappeared and the typical law required that the procedure actually be necessary for that purpose.

Gradually, in the middle and late 19th century the quickening distinction disappeared from the statutory law of most States and the degree of the offense and the penalties were increased. By the end of the 1950's, a large majority of the jurisdictions banned abortion, however and whenever performed, unless done to save or preserve the life of the mother. The exceptions, Alabama and the District of Columbia, permitted abortion to preserve the mother's health. Three States permitted abortions that were not "unlawfully" performed or that were not "without lawful justification," leaving interpretation of those standards to the courts. In the past several years, however, a trend toward liberalization of abortion statutes has resulted in adoption, by about one-third of the States, of less stringent laws, most of them patterned after the ALI Model Penal Code, §230.3, set forth as Appendix B to the opinion in Doe v Bolton, 410 US 205, 35 L Ed 2d 201.

It is thus apparent that in common law, at the time of the adoption of our Constitution, and throughout the major portion of the 19th century, abortion was viewed with less disfavor than under most American statutes currently in effect. Phrasing it another way, a woman enjoyed a substantially broader right to terminate a pregnancy than she does in most States today. At least with respect to the early stage of pregnancy, and very possibly without such a limitation, the opportunity to make this choice was present in this country well into the 19th century. Even later, the law continued for some time to treat less punitively an abortion procured in early pregnancy.

6. *The position of the American Medical Association.* The anti-abortion mood prevalent in this country in the late 19th century was shared by the medical profession. Indeed, the attitude of the profession may have played a significant role in the enactment of stringent criminal abortion legislation during that period.

An AMA Committee on Criminal Abortion was appointed in May 1857. It presented its report, 12 Trans of the Am Med Assn 73-78 (1859), to the Twelfth Annual Meeting. That report observed that the Committee had been appointed to investigate criminal abortion "with a view to its general suppression." It deplored abortion and its frequency and it listed three causes of "this general demoralization":

"The first of these causes is a wide-spread popular ignorance of the true character of the crime--a belief, even among mothers themselves, that the foetus is not alive till after the period of quickening.
"The second of the agents alluded to is the fact that the profession themselves are frequently supposed careless of foetal life....
"The third reason of the frightful extent of this crime is found in the grave defects of our laws, both common and

statute, as regards the independent and actual existence of
the child before birth, as living being. These errors,
which are sufficient in most instances to prevent conviction, are based, and only based, upon mistaken and exploded
medical dogmas. With strange inconsistency, the law fully
acknowledges the foetus in utero and its inherent rights,
for civil purposes; while personally and as criminally affected, it fails to recognize it, and to its life as yet
denies all protection."

The Committee then offered, and the Association adopted,
resolutions protesting "against such unwarrantable destruction
of human life," calling upon state legislatures to revise their
abortion laws, and requesting the cooperation of state medical
societies "in pressing the subject."

In 1871 a long and vivid report was submitted by the Committee on Criminal Abortion. It ended with the observation, "We
had to deal with human life. In a matter of less importance we
could entertain no compromise. An honest judge on the bench
would call things by their proper names. We could do no less."
22 Trans of the Am Med Assn 258 (1871). It proffered resolutions, adopted by the Association, id., at 38-39, recommending,
among other things, that it "be unlawful and unprofessional for
any physician to induce abortion or premature labor, without the
concurrent opinion of at least one respectable consulting physician, and then always with a view to the safety of the child--if
that be possible," and calling "the attention of the clergy of
all denominations to the perverted views of morality entertained
by a large class of females--aye, and men also, on this important question."

Except for periodic condemnation of the criminal abortion-
ist, no further formal AMA action took place until 1967. In
that year, the Committee on Human Reproduction urged the adoption of a stated policy of opposition to induced abortion,
except when there is "documented medical evidence" of a threat
to the health or life of the mother, or that the child "may be
born with incapacitating physical deformity or mental deficiency," or that a pregnancy "resulting from legally established
statutory or forcible rape or incest may constitute a threat to
the mental or physical health of the patient," and two other
physicians "chosen because of their recognized professional competence have examined the patient and have concurred in writing,"
and the procedure "is performed in a hospital accredited by the
Joint Commission on Accreditation of Hospitals." The providing
of medical information by physicians to state legislatures in
their consideration of legislation regarding therapeutic abortion was "to be considered consistent with the principles of
ethics of the American Medical Association." This recommendation was adopted by the House of Delegates.

In 1970, after the introduction of a variety of proposed resolutions, and of a report from its Board of Trustees, a reference committee noted "polarization of the medical profession on
this controversial issue"; division among those who had testified; a difference of opinion among AMA councils and committees;
"the remarkable shift in testimony" in six months, felt to be
influenced "by the rapid changes in state laws and by the judicial decisions which tend to make abortion more freely available;" and a feeling "that this trend will continue." On June
25, 1970, the House of Delegates adopted preambles and most of
the resolutions proposed by the reference committee. The preambles emphasized "the best interests of the patient," "sound
clinical judgment," and "informed patient consent," in contrast
to "mere acquiescence to the patient's demand." The resolutions
asserted that abortion is a medical procedure that should be
performed by a licensed physician in an accredited hospital only
after consultation with two other physicians and in conformity
with state law, and that no party to the procedure should be required to violate personally held moral principles. Proceedings
of the AMA House of Delegates 220 (June 1970). The AMA Judicial
Council rendered a complementary opinion.

     7. *The position of the American Public Health Association.*
In October 1970, the Executive Board of the APHA adopted Standards for Abortion Services. These were five in number:

> "a.  Rapid and simple abortion referral must be readily
> available through state and local public health departments,
> medical societies, or other nonprofit organizations.
> "b.  An important function of counseling should be to
> simplify and expedite the provision of abortion services; it
> should not delay the obtaining of these services.
> "c.  Psychiatric consultation should not be mandatory.
> As in the case of other specialized medical services, psy-
> chiatric consultation should be sought for definite indica-
> tions and not on a routine basis.
> "d.  A wide range of individuals from appropriately
> trained, sympathetic volunteers to highly skilled physicians
> may qualify as abortion counselors.
> "e.  Contraception and/or sterilization should be dis-
> cussed with each abortion patient."

It was recommended that abortions in the second trimester
and early abortions in the presence of existing medical complications be performed in hospitals as inpatient procedures. For
pregnancies in the first trimester, abortion in the hospital
with or without overnight stay "is probably the safest practice."
An abortion in an extramural facility, however, is an acceptable
alternative "provided arrangements exist in advance to admit
patients promptly if unforeseen complications develop." Standards for an abortion facility were listed. It was said that

at present abortions should be performed by physicians or os-
teopaths who are licensed to practice and who have "adequate
training."

Three reasons have been advanced to explain historically the
enactment of criminal abortion laws in the 19th century and to
justify their continued existence.

It has been argued occasionally that these laws were the
product of a Victorian social concern to discourage illicit
sexual conduct. Texas, however, does not advance this justification in the present case, and it appears that no court or
commentator has taken the argument seriously. The appellants
and amici contend, moreover, that this is not a proper state
purpose at all and suggest that, if it were, the Texas statutes
are overbroad in protecting it since the law fails to distin-
quish between married and unwed mothers.

A second reason is concerned with abortion as a medical procedure. When most criminal abortion laws were first enacted,
the procedure was a hazardous one for the woman. This was particularly true prior to the development of antisepsis. Anti-
septic techniques, of course, were based on discoveries by
Lister, Pasteur, and others first announced in 1867, but were
not generally accepted and employed until about the turn of the
century. Abortion mortality was high. Even after 1900, and
perhaps until as late as the development of antibiotics in the
1940's, standard modern techniques such as dilation and curet-
tage were not nearly so safe as they are today. Thus, it has
been argued that a State's real concern in enacting a criminal
abortion law was to protect the pregnant woman, that is, to
restrain her from submitting to a procedure that placed her
life in serious jeopardy.

Modern medical techniques have altered this situation. Appellants and various amici refer to medical data indicating
that abortion in early pregnancy, this is, prior to the end of
the first trimester, although not without its risk, is now
relatively safe. Mortality rates for women undergoing early
abortions, where the procedure is legal, appear to be as low as
or lower than the rates for normal childbirth. Consequently,
any interest of the State in protecting the woman from an inherently hazardous procedure, except when it would be equally
dangerous for her to forgo it, has largely disappeared. Of
course, important state interests in the area of health and
medical standards do remain.

The State has a legitimate interest in seeing to it that
abortion, like any other medical procedure, is performed under
circumstances that insure maximum safety for the patient. This
interest obviously extends at least to the performing physician
and his staff, to the facilities involved, to the availability
of aftercare, and to adequate provision for any complication
or emergency that might arise. The prevalence of high

mortality rates at illegal "abortion mills" strengthens, rather than weakens, the State's interest in regulating the conditions under which abortions are performed. Moreover, the risk to the woman increases as her pregnancy continues. Thus, the State retains a definite interest in protecting the woman's own health and safety when an abortion is proposed at a late stage of pregnancy.

The third reason is the State's interest--some phrase it in terms of duty--in protecting prenatal life. Some of the argument for this justification rests on the theory that a new human life is present from the moment of conception. The State's interest and general obligation to protect life then extends, it is argued, to prenatal life. Only when the life of the pregnant mother herself is at stake, balanced against the life she carries within her, should the interest of the embryo or fetus not prevail. Logically, of course, a legitimate state interest in this area need not stand or fall on acceptance of the belief that life begins at conception or at some other point prior to live birth. In assessing the State's interest, recognition may be given to the less rigid claim that as long as at least *potential* life is involved, the State may assert interests beyond the protection of the pregnant woman alone.

Parties challenging state abortion laws have sharply disputed in some courts the contention that a purpose of these laws, when enacted, was to protect prenatal life. Pointing to the absence of legislative history to support the contention, they claim that most state laws were designed solely to protect the woman. Because medical advances have lessened this concern, at least with respect to abortion in early pregnancy, they argue that with respect to such abortions the laws can no longer be justified by any state interest. There is some scholarly support for this view of original purpose. The few state courts called upon to interpret their laws in the late 19th and early 20th centuries did focus on the State's interest in protecting the woman's health rather than in preserving the embryo and fetus. Proponents of this view point out that in many States, including Texas, by statute or judicial interpretation, the pregnant woman herself could not be prosecuted for self-abortion or for cooperating in an abortion performed upon her by another. They claim that adoption of the "quickening" distinction through received common law and state statutes tacitly recognizes the greater health hazzards inherent in late abortion and impliedly repudiates the theory that life begins at conception.

It is with these interests, and the weight to be attached to them, that this case is concerned.

The Constitution does not explicitly mention any right of privacy. In a line of decisions, however, going back perhaps as far as Union Pacific R. Co. v Botsford, 141 US 250, 251 (1891), the Court has recognized that a right of personal privacy, or a

guarantee of certain areas or zones of privacy, does exist under
the Constitution.  In varying contexts, the Court or individual
Justices have, indeed, found at least the roots of that right in
the First Amendment, Stanley v Georgia, 394 US 557, 564 (1969);
in the Fourth and Fifth Amendments, Terry v Ohio; in the penumbras of the Bill of Rights, Griswold v Connecticut, 381 US, at
484-485, in the Ninth Amendment, id., at 486, 14 L Ed 2d 510
(Goldberg, J., concurring); or in the concept of liberty guaranteed by the first section of the Fourteenth Amendment, see Meyer
v Nebraska, 262 US 390, 399 (1923).  These decisions make it
clear that only personal rights that can be deemed "fundamental"
or "implicit in the concept of ordered liberty," Palko v Connecticut, 302 US 319, 325, 82 L Ed 288, 58 S Ct 149 (1937), are included in this guarantee of personal privacy.  They also make it
clear that the right has some extension to activities relating
to marriage, Loving v Virginia, 388 US 1, 12 (1967); procreation, Skinner v Oklahoma, 316 US 535 (1942); contraception,
Eisenstadt v Baird, 405 US, at 453-454; family relationships,
Prince v Massachusetts, 321 US 158, 166 (1944); and child
rearing and education, Pierce v Society of Sisters, 268 US 510,
535.  This right of privacy, whether it be founded in the Fourteenth Amendment's concept of personal liberty and restrictions
upon state action, as we feel it is, or, as the District Court
determined, in the Ninth Amendment's reservation of rights to
the people, is broad enough to encompass a woman's decision
whether or not to terminate her pregnancy.  The detriment that
the State would impose upon the pregnant woman by denying this
choice altogether is apparent.  Specific and direct harm medically diagnosable even in early pregnancy may be involved.  Ma-
ternity, or additional offspring, may force upon the women a
distressful life and future.  Psychological harm may be imminent.
Mental and physical health may be taxed by child care.  There is
also the distress, for all concerned, associated with the unwanted child, and there is the problem of bringing a child into
a family already unable, psychologically and otherwise, to care
for it.  In other cases, as in this one, the additional difficul-
ties and continuing stigma of unwed motherhood may be involved.
All these are factors the woman and her responsible physician
necessarily will consider in consultation.

On the basis of elements such as these, appellant and some
amici argue that the woman's right is absolute and that she is
entitled to terminate her pregnancy at whatever time, in whatever way, and for whatever reason she alone chooses.  With this
we do not agree.  Appellant's arguments that Texas either has no
valid interest at all in regulating the abortion decision, or no
interest strong enough to support any limitation upon the woman's sole determination, is unpersuasive.  The Court's decisions
recognizing a right of privacy also acknowledge that some state
regulation in areas protected by that right is appropriate.  As
noted above, a State may properly assert important interests in

safeguarding health, in maintaining medical standards, and in
protecting potential life.  At some point in pregnancy, these
respective interests become sufficiently compelling to sustain
regulation of the factors that govern the abortion decision.
The privacy right involved, therefore, cannot be said to be absolute.  In fact, it is not clear to us that the claim asserted
by some amici that one has an unlimited right to do with one's
body as one pleases bears a close relationship to the right of
privacy previously articulated in the Court's decisions.  The
Court has refused to recognize an unlimited right of this kind
in the past.

We, therefore, conclude that the right of personal privacy
includes the abortion decision, but that this right is not unqualified and must be considered against important state interests in regulation.

We note that those federal and state courts that have recently considered abortion law challenges have reached the same
conclusion.  A majority, in addition to the District Court in
the present case, have held state laws unconstitutional, at
least in part, because of vagueness or because of overbreadth
and abridgment of rights.

Others have sustained state statutes.

Although the results are divided, most of these courts have
agreed that the right of privacy, however based, is broad enough
to cover the abortion decision; that the right, nonetheless, is
not absolute and is subject to some limitations; and that at
some point the state interests as to protection of health, medical standards, and prenatal life, become dominant.  We agree
with this approach.

Where certain "fundamental rights" are involved, the Court
has held that regulation limiting these rights may be justified
only by a "compelling state interest," and that legislative en-
actments must be narrowly drawn to express only the legitimate
state interests at stake.

In the recent abortion cases, cited above, courts have recognized these principles.  Those striking down state laws have
generally scrutinized the State's interest in protecting health
and potential life, and have concluded that neither interest
justified broad limitations on the reasons for which a physician
and his pregnant patient might decide that she should have an
abortion in the early stages of pregnancy.  Courts sustaining
state laws have held that the State's determinations to protect
health or prenatal life are dominant and constitutionally justifiable.

The District Court held that the appellee failed to meet his burden of demonstrating that the Texas statute's infringement upon Roe's rights was necessary to support a compelling state interest, and that, although the appellee presented "several compelling justifications for state presence in the area of abortions," the statutes outstripped these justifications and swept "far beyond any areas of compelling state interest." 314 F Supp, at 1222-1223. Appellant and appellee both contest that holding. Appellant, as has been indicated, claims an absolute right that bars any state imposition of criminal penalties in the area. Appellee argues that the State's determination to recognize and protect prenatal life from and after conception constitutes a compelling state interest. As noted above, we do not agree fully with either formulation.

A. The appellee and certain amici argue that the fetus is a "person" within the language and meaning of the Fourteenth Amendment and meaning of the Fourteenth Amendment. In support of this, they outline at length and in detail the well-known facts of fetal development. If this suggestion of personhood is established, the appellant's case, of course, collapses, for the fetus' right to life is then guaranteed specifically by the Amendment. The appellant conceded as much on reargument. On the other hand, the appellee conceded on reargument that no case could be cited that holds a fetus is a person within the meaning of the Fourteenth Amendment.

The Constitution does not define "person" in so many words. Section 1 of the Fourteenth Amendment contains three references to "person." The first, in defining "citizens," speaks of "persons born or naturalized in the United States." The word also appears both in the Due Process Clause and in the Equal Protection Clause. "Person" is used in other places in the Constitution:

But in nearly all these instances, the use of the word is such that it has application only postnatally. None indicates, with any assurance, that it has any possible prenatal application.

All this, together with our observation, supra, that throughout the major portion of the 19th century prevailing legal abortion practices were far freer than they are today, persuades us that the word "person," as used in the Fourteenth Amendment, does not include the unborn. This is in accord with the results reached in those few cases where the issue has been squarely presented. Indeed, our decision in United States v Vuitch, 402 US 62 (1971), inferentially is to the same effect, for we there would not have indulged in statutory interpretation favorable to abortion in specified circumstances if the necessary consequence was the termination of life entitled to Fourteenth Amendment protection.

This conclusion, however, does not of itself fully answer the contentions raised by Texas, and we pass on to other considerations.

B.  The pregnant woman cannot be isolated in her privacy. She carries an embryo and, later, a fetus, if one accepts the medical definitions of the developing young in the human uterus. See Dorland's Illustrated Medical Dictionary 478-479, 547 (24th ed 1965).  The situation therefore is inherently different from marital intimacy, or bedroom possession of obscene material, or marriage, or procreation, or education, with which Eisenstadt, Griswold,  Stanley, Loving, Skinner, Pierce, and Meyer were respectively concerned.  As we have intimated above, it is reasonable and appropriate for a State to decide that at some point in time another interest, that of health of the mother or that of potential human life, becomes significantly involved.  The woman's privacy is no longer sole and any right of privacy she possesses must be measured accordingly.

Texas urges that, apart from the Fourteenth Amendment, life begins at conception and is present throught pregnancy, and that, therefore, the State has a compelling interest in protecting that life from and after conception.  We need not resolve the difficult question of when life begins.  When those trained in the respective disciplines of medicine, philosophy, and theology are unable to arrive at any consensus, the judicatory, at this point in the development of man's knowledge, is not in a position to speculate as to the answer.

It should be sufficient to note briefly the wide divergence of thinking on this most sensitive and difficult question.  There has always been strong support for the view that life does not begin until live birth.  This was the belief of the Stoics.  It appears to be the predominant, though not the unanimous, attitude of the Jewish faith.  It may be taken to represent also the position of a large segment of the Protestant community, insofar as that can be ascertained; organized groups that have taken a formal position on the abortion issue have generally regarded abortion as a matter for the conscience of the individual and her family.  As we have noted, the common law found greater significance in quickening.  Physicians and their scientific colleagues have regarded that event with less interest and have tended to focus either upon conception, upon live birth, or upon the interim point at which the fetus becomes "viable," that is, potentially able to live outside the mother's womb, albeit with artificial aid.  Viability is usually placed at about seven months (28 weeks) but may occur earlier, even at 24 weeks.  The Aristotelian theory of "mediate animation," that held sway throughout the Middle Ages and the Renaissance in Europe, continued to be official Roman Catholic dogma until the 19th century, despite opposition to this "ensoulment" theory from those in the Church who would recognize the existence of life from the moment of conception.  The latter is now, of course, the official belief of the Catholic Church.  As one of the briefs amicus discloses, this is a view strongly held by many non-Catholics as well, and by many physicians.  Substantial problems for precise

definition of this view are posed, however, by new embryological
data that purport to indicate that conception is a "process"
over time, rather than an event, and by new medical techniques
such as menstrual extraction, the "morning-after" pill, implantation of embryos, artificial insemination, and even artificial
wombs.

In areas other than criminal abortion, the law has been re-
luctant to endorse any theory that life, as we recognize it,
begins before live birth or to accord legal rights to the unborn
except in narrowly defined situations and except when the rights
are contingent upon live birth. For example, the traditional
rule of tort law denied recovery for prenatal injuries even
though the child was born alive. That rule has been changed in
almost every jurisdiction. In most States, recovery is said to
be permitted only if the fetus was viable, or at least quick,
when the injuries were sustained, though few courts have squarely so held. In a recent development, generally opposed by the
commentators, some States permit the parents of a stillborn
child to maintain an action for wrongful death because of prenatal injuries. Such an action, however, would appear to be one
to vindicate the parents' interest and is thus consistent with
the view that the fetus, at most, represents only the potentiality of life. Similarly, unborn children have been recognized
as acquiring rights or interests by way of inheritance or other
devolution of property, and have been represented by guardians
ad litem. Perfection of the interests involved, again, has
generally been contingent upon live birth. In short, the unborn
have never been recognized in the law as persons in the whole
sense.

In view of all this, we do not agree that, by adopting one
theory of life, Texas may override the rights of the pregnant
woman that are at stake. We repeat, however, that the State
does have an important and legitimate interest in preserving
and protecting the health of the pregnant woman, whether she be
a resident of the State or a nonresident who seeks medical consultation and treatment there, and that it has still *another*
important and legitimate interest in protecting the potentiality
of human life. These interests are separate and distinct. Each
grows in substantiality as the woman approaches term and, at a
point during pregnancy, each becomes "compelling."

With respect to the State's important and legitimate interest in the health of the mother, the "compelling" point, in the
light of present medical knowledge, is at approximately the end
of the first trimester. This is so because of the now-
established medical fact, referred to above at 149, 35 L Ed 2d,
174, 175, that until the end of the first trimester mortality
in abortion may be less than mortality in normal childbirth. It
follows that, from and after this point, a State may regulate
the abortion procedure to the extent that the regulation

reasonably relates to the preservation and protection of maternal health.  Examples of permissible state regulation in this area are requirements as to the qualifications of the person who is to perform the abortion; as to the licensure of that person; as to the facility in which the procedure is to be performed, that is, whether it must be a hospital or may be a clinic or some other place of less-than-hospital status; as to the licensing of the facility; and the like.

This means, on the other hand, that, for the period of pregnancy prior to this "compelling" point, the attending physician, in consultation with his patient, is free to determine without regulation by the State, that, in his medical judgment, the patient's pregnancy should be terminated.  If that decision is reached, the judgment may be effectuated by an abortion free of interference by the State.

With respect to the State's important and legitimate interest in potential life, the "compelling" point is at viability.  This is so because the fetus then presumably has the capability of meaningful life outside the mother's womb.  State regulation protective of fetal life after viability thus has both logical and biological justifications.  If the State is interested in protecting fetal life after viability, it may go so far as to proscribe abortion during that period, except when it is necessary to preserve the life or health of the mother.

Measured against these standards, Art 1196 of the Texas Penal Code, in restricting legal abortions to those "procured or attempted by medical advice for the purpose of saving the life of the mother," sweeps too broadly.  The statute makes no distinction between abortions performed early in pregnancy and those performed later, and it limits to a single reason, "saving" the mother's life, the legal justification for the procedure.  The statute, therefore, cannot survive the constitutional attack made upon it here.

This conclusion makes it unnecessary for us to consider the additional challenge to the Texas statute asserted on grounds of vagueness.

To summarize and to repeat:
1.  A state criminal abortion statute of the current Texas type, that excepts from criminality only a *life-saving* procedure on behalf of the mother, without regard to pregnancy stage and without recognition of the other interests involved, is violative of the Due Process Clause of the Fourteenth Amendment.
(a)  For the stage prior to approximately the end of the first trimester, the abortion decision and its effectuation must be left to the medical judgment of the pregnant woman's attending physician.
(b)  For the stage subsequent to approximately the end of the first trimester, the State, in promoting its interest in the health of the mother, may, if it chooses, regulate the abortion procedure in ways that are reasonably related to maternal health.

(c)  For the stage subsequent to viability, the State in promoting its interest in the potentiality of human life may, if it chooses, regulate, and even proscribe, abortion except where it is necessary, in appropriate medical judgment, for the preservation of the life or health of the mother.

2.  The State may define the term "physician," as it has been employed in the preceding numbered paragraphs of this Part XI of this opinion, to mean only a physician currently licensed by the State, and may proscribe any abortion by a person who is not a physician as so defined.

In Doe v Bolton, 410 US 179 procedural requirements contained in one of the modern abortion statutes are considered. That opinion and this one, of course, are to be read together.

This holding, we feel, is consistent with the relative weights of the respective interests involved, with the lessons and examples of medical and legal history, with the lenity of the common law, and with the demands of the profound problems of the present day.  The decision leaves the State free to place increasing restrictions on abortion as the period of pregnancy lengthens, so long as those restrictions are tailored to the recognized state interests.  The decision vindicates the right of the physician to administer medical treatment according to his professional judgment up to the points where important state interests provide compelling justifications for intervention. Up to those points, the abortion decision in all its aspects is inherently, and primarily, a medical decision, and basic responsibility for it must rest with the physician.  If an individual practitioner abuses the privilege of exercising proper medical judgment, the usual remedies, judicial and intra-professional, are available.

Our conclusion that Art 1196 is unconstitutional means, of course, that the Texas abortion statutes, as a unit must fall. The exception of Art 1196 cannot be stricken separately, for then the State would be left with a statute proscribing all abortion procedures no matter how medically urgent the case.

Although the District Court granted plaintiff Roe declaratory relief, it stopped short of issuing an injunction against enforcement of the Texas statutes.  The Court has recognized that different considerations enter into a federal court's decision as to declaratory relief, on the one hand, and injunctive relief, on the other.  We are not dealing with a statute that, on its face, appears to abridge free expression, an area of particular concern under Dombrowski and refined in Younger v Harris, 401 US, at 50.

We find it unnecessary to decide whether the District Court erred in withholding injunctive relief, for we assume the Texas prosecutorial authorities will give full credence to this decision that the present criminal abortion statutes of that State are unconstitutional.

The judgment of the District Court as to intervenor Hallford is reversed, and Dr. Hallford's complaint in intervention is dismissed. In all other respects, the judgment of the District Court is affirmed. Costs are allowed to the appellee.
It is so ordered.

b. *Griswold v. Connecticut,* 381 U.S. 479 (1965)

The Supreme Court found it unconstitutional for a state to make use of the contraceptive by married persons a crime and to punish someone who provides married persons with information concerning their use for the crime of aiding and abetting them. The court found a "zone of privacy created by several fundamental constitutional guarantees" which involved at least those intimate aspects of married life including decisions to bear a child. Justice Douglas was also outraged by the way such a law might be enforced: "Would we allow the police to search the sacred precincts of marital bedrooms for tell-tale signs of the use of contraceptives?" Not if contraceptives are related to intimate personal choices.

c. *Eisenstadt v. Baird,* 405 U.S. 438 (1972)

In Baird the court makes it clear that reproductive autonomy is the interest most at stake and least susceptible to governmental intrusion. A state statute forbidding the dispensing of contraceptives to unmarried individuals was striken down as a violation of such autonomy:

If the right of privacy means anything, it is the right of the individual, married or single, to be free from unwarranted governmental intrusion into matters so fundamentally affecting a person as the decision whether to bear or beget a child.

d. _Doe v. Bolton,_ 410 U.S. 179 (1973)

Whereas after the first trimester the state may regulate
abortion procedures to insure the health and safety of the pregnant woman, it may not require abortions to be performed only
with the approval of a second physician or review committee or
with the approval of anyone else other than the woman's personal
physician.

e. _Planned Parenthood of Missouri v. Danforth,_   428 U.S.
   52 (1976)

In the wake of Roe v. Wade many states passed restrictive
abortion statutes.  The first such statute to be reviewed by the
Supreme Court was Missouri's.  It reads as follows:

SECTION 1.  It is the intention of the general assembly of
the state of Missouri to reasonably regulate abortion in confor-
mance with the decisions of the supreme court of the United
States.
SECTION 2.  Unless the language or context clearly indicates
a different meaning is intended, the following words or phrases
for the purpose of this act shall be given the meaning ascribed
to them:
(1)  "Abortion," the intentional destruction of the life of
an embryo or fetus in his or her mother's womb or the intentional termination of the pregnancy of a mother with an intention other than to increase the probability of a live birth or
to remove a dead or dying unborn child;
(2)  "Viability," that stage of fetal development when the
life of the unborn child may be continued indefinitely outside
the womb by natural or artificial life-supportive systems;
(3)  "Physician," any person licensed to practice medicine
in this state by the state board of registration of the healing
arts.
SECTION 3.  No abortion shall be performed prior to the end
of the first twelve weeks of pregnancy except:
(1) By a duly licensed, consenting physician in the exercise
of his best clinical medical judgment.
(2) After the woman, prior to submitting to the abortion,
certifies in writing her consent to the abortion and that her
consent is informed and freely given and is not the result of
coercion.

(3) With the written consent of the woman's spouse, unless the abortion is certified by a licensed physician to be necessary in order to preserve the life of the mother.

(4) With the written consent of one parent or person in loco parentis of the woman if the woman is unmarried and under the age of eighteen years, unless the abortion is certified by a licensed physician as necessary in order to preserve the life of the mother.

SECTION 4.  No abortion performed subsequent to the first twelve weeks of pregnancy shall be performed except where the provisions of section 3 of this act are satisfied and in a hospital.

SECTION 5.  No abortion not necessary to preserve the life or health of the mother shall be performed unless the attending physician first certifies with reasonable medical certainty that the fetus is not viable.

SECTION 6.  (1) No person who performs or induces an abortion shall fail to exercise that degree of professional skill, care and diligence to preserve the life and health of the fetus which such person would be required to exercise in order to preserve the life and health of any fetus intended to be born and not aborted.  Any physician or person assisting in the abortion who shall fail to take such measures to encourage or to sustain the life of the child, and the death of the child results, shall be deemed guilty of manslaughter and upon conviction shall be punished as provided in Section 559.140, RSMo.  Further, such physician or other person shall be liable in an action for damages as provided in Section 537.080, RSMo.

(2) Whoever, with intent to do so, shall take the life of a premature infant aborted alive, shall be guilty of murder of the second degree.

(3) No person shall use any fetus or premature infant aborted alive for any type of scientific, research, laboratory or other kind of experimentation either prior to or subsequent to any abortion procedure except as necessary to protect or preserve the life and health of such premature infant aborted alive.

SECTION 7.  In every case where a live born infant results from an attempted abortion which was not performed to save the life or health of the mother, such infant shall be an abandoned ward of the state under the jurisdiction of the juvenile court wherein the abortion occurred, and the mother and father, if he consented to the abortion, of such infant shall have no parental rights or obligations whatsoever relating to such infant, as if the parental rights had been terminated pursuant to section 211.411, RSMo.  The attending physician shall forthwith notify said juvenile court of the existence of such live born infant.

SECTION 8.  Any woman seeking an abortion in the state of Missouri shall be verbally informed of the provisions of section 7 of this act by the attending physician and the woman shall certify in writing that she has been so informed.

SECTION 9.  The general assembly finds that the method or technique of abortion known as saline amniocentesis whereby the amniotic fluid is withdrawn and a saline or other fluid is inserted into the amniotic sac for the purpose of killing the fetus and artificially inducing labor is deleterious to maternal health and is hereby prohibited after the first twelve weeks of pregnancy.

SECTION 10.  (1) Every health facility and physician shall be supplied with forms promulgated by the division of health, the purpose and function of which shall be the preservation of maternal health and life by adding to the sum of medical knowledge through the compilation of relevant maternal health and life data and to monitor all abortions performed to assure that they are done only under and in accordance with the provisions of the law.

(2) The forms shall be provided by the state division of health.

(3) All information obtained by physician, hospital, clinic or other health facility from a patient for the purpose of preparing reports to the division of health under this section or reports received by the division of health shall be confidential and shall be used only for statistical purposes.  Such records, however, may be inspected and health data acquired by local, state, or national public health officers.

SECTION 11.  All medical records and other documents required to be kept shall be maintained in the permanent files of the health facility in which the abortion was performed for a period of seven years.

SECTION 12.  Any practitioner of medicine, surgery, or nursing, or other health personnel who shall willfully and knowingly do or assist any actions made unlawful by this act shall be subject to having his license, application for license, or authority to practice his profession as a physician, surgeon, or nurse in the state of Missouri rejected or revoked by the appropriate state licensing board.

SECTION 13.  Any physician or other person who fails to maintain the confidentiality of any records or reports required under this act is guilty of a misdemeanor and, upon conviction, shall be punished as provided by law.

SECTION 14.  Any person who contrary to the provisions of this act knowingly performs or aids in the performance of any abortion or knowingly fails to perform any action required by this act shall be guilty of a misdemeanor and, upon conviction, shall be punished as provided by law.

SECTION 15.  Any person who is not a licensed physician as defined in section 2 of this act who performs or attempts to perform an abortion on another as defined in subdivision (1) of section 2 of this act, is guilty of a felony, and upon conviction, shall be imprisoned by the department of corrections for a term of not less than two years nor more than seventeen years.

SECTION 16.  Nothing in this act shall be construed to
exempt any person, firm, or corporation from civil liability
for medical malpractice for negligent acts or certification
under this act.

SECTION A.  Because of the necessity for immediate state
action to regulate abortions to protect the lives and health of
citizens of this state, this act is deemed necessary for the immediate preservation of the public health, welfare, peace and
safety, and is hereby declared to be an emergency act within the
meaning of the constitution, and this act shall be in full force
and effect upon its passage and approval.

SECTION B.  If any provision of this Act or the application
thereof to any person or circumstance shall be held invalid,
such invalidity does not affect the provisions or application
of this Act which can be given effect without the invalid provision or application, and to this end the provisions of this
Act are declared to be severable.

Approved June 14, 1974.
Effective June 14, 1974.

The Court reached the following conclusions concerning the

statute:

1.  "Viability" can be constitutionally defined as "that

stage of fetal development when the life of the unborn child may

be continued indefinitely outside the womb by natural or artifi-

cial life-supportive systems" and the application of such a def-

inition "must be a matter for the judgment of the responsible

attending physician."

2.  A state may constitutionally require a woman to give her

informed, voluntary and written consent to the abortion prior to

its being performed.

3.  A state may not constitutionally require the consent of

a spouse to an abortion during the first trimester because "it

is the woman who physically bears the child and who is more

directly  and immediately affected by the pregnancy."

4. A state may not constitutionally require the consent of a minor's parent or parents to an abortion during the first trimester, but a properly worded notice requirement might be acceptable.

5. A state may not proscribe a method of abortion (saline amniocentesis) that is employed by a majority of physicians and is safer than continuing a pregnancy to term.

6. A state may require certain records concerning all abortions to be kept "for the advancement of medical knowledge" so long as they are kept "confidential."

7. A state cannot constitutionally require a physician to attempt to preserve the life of a fetus delivered during an abortion until after viability has been reached.

All nine justices agreed with points 1, 2, and 6; points 3, 5, and 7 were decided by a 6-3 margin; and issue 4, on parental consent, was decided by a 5-4 margin.

### f. *Bellotti v. Baird*,  443 U.S. 622 (1979)

The Court found a Massachusetts law that required parental consent for abortion of pregnant minors, without offering any alternatives, unconstitutional, since it gave the parents something the state did not have to give:  veto power over a woman's decision to have an abortion.

g.  _H.L. v. Matheson_, 101 S. Ct. 1164 (1981)

The Court upheld a Utah statute requiring a physician "to
notify, if possible" the parents or guardian of a pregnant minor
before performing an abortion.  The case applied to "immature"
minors and the Court saw the decision as promoting family integrity by encouraging parental consultation and allowing parents
the opportunity to supply essential medical and other information to the physician.


2.  State Statutes

By 1981, fewer than half of the states had availed themselves of the option of regulating the availability of an abortion after viability.  Seventeen states prohibited all post-
viability abortions except those necessary to preserve the life
or health of the mother:  Fla. Stat. Ann. § 458.225 (West Supp.
1979); Ill. Ann. Stat. ch. 38, § 81-25 (Smith-Hurd Supp. 1979);
Ind. Code Ann. § 35-1-58.5-2 (Burns 1979); Iowa Code (Special
Pamphlet 1979); Ky. Rev. Stat. § 311.780 (1978); La. Rev. Stat.
Ann. § 40.1299.35.4 (West Supp. 1979); Me. Rev. Stat. Ann. tit.
22, § 1598 (1964); Minn. Stat. Ann. § 145-412 (West Supp. 1979);
Mo. Ann. Stat. § 188.030 (Vernon Supp. 1979); Mont. Rev. Codes
Ann. § 50-20-109 (1978); Neb.  Rev. Stat. § 28-329 (1978); N.D.
Cent. Code § 14-02.1-03 (Interim Supp. 1979); Okla. Stat. Ann.
tit. 63, § 1-732 (West Supp. 1978-1979); 35 Pa. Cons. Stat. Ann.
§ 6606 (Purdon 1977); Tenn. Code Ann. § 39-301 (1975); Utah Code

Ann. § 76-302 (1978); Wyo. Stat. § 35-6-102 (1977).  Five others
proscribed abortions after a particular date:  N.C. Gen. Stat.
§ 14-45.1 (Supp. 1979) (twenty weeks); Mass. Gen. Laws Ann. ch.
112, § 12M (West. Supp. 1979) (twenty-four weeks); Nev. Rev.
Stat. § 442.250 (1973)(twenty-four weeks); S.D. Comp. Laws Ann.
§ 34-23A-5 (1977) (twenty-four weeks); N.Y. Penal Law § 125.05
(McKinney 1975) (twenty-four weeks).

Five states have passed legislation requiring the availability of specific medical resources during the abortion of a
viable fetus in order to promote fetal survival.  Massachusetts
and North Dakota require the presence of life-support equipment:
Mass. Gen. Law Ann. ch. 112, § 12 (West Supp. 1979); N.D. Cent.
Code of 14-02.1-05 (Sup. 1979).  Louisiana and Oklahoma require
that a physician be present during the abortion to care for the
fetus:  La. Rev. Stat. Ann. § 40-1299. 35.4 (West Supp. 1979);
Okla. Stat. Ann. Tit. 63, § 1-732 (West Supp. 1979).  Indiana
requires that the abortion facility contain an intensive care
unit for premature infants:  Ind. Code Ann. § 35-1-58.5-7 (Burns
1979).

### 3.  "Human Life" Amendments

A constitutional amendment can make abortion illegal.  There
are two mechanisms for amending the constitution.  The first
requires a two-thirds vote of both houses and ratification by
thirty-eight state legislatures.  The second method requires
that thirty-four states pass resolutions calling for a consti-

tutional convention and, again, that the amendment be ratified

by thirty-eight state legislatures.  Currently, nineteen of the

requisite thirty-four states have called for a constitutional

convention.  They are Alabama, Arkansas, Delaware, Idaho,

Indiana, Kentucky, Louisiana, Massachusetts, Mississippi,

Missouri, Nebraska, Nevada, New Jersey, Oklahoma, Pennsylvania,

Rhode Island, South Dakota, Tennessee, and Utah.  There are

several proposed human life amendments.  Reproduced below is

that of the National Right to Life Committee.

### a.  "Human Life" Amendment Proposed by the National Right to Life Committee

Section 1.  The right to life is the paramount and most
fundamental right of a person.
Section 2.  With respect to the right to life guaranteed
to persons by the fifth and fourteenth articles of amendment to
the Constitution, the word "person" applies to all human beings,
irrespective of age, health, function, or condition of depen-
dency, including their unborn offspring at every stage of biological development including fertilization.
Section 3.  No unborn person shall be deprived of life by
any person; Provided, however, That nothing in this article
shall prohibit a law permitting only those medical procedures
required to prevent the death of a pregnant woman; but this law
must require every reasonable effort be made to preserve the
life and health of the unborn child.
Section 4.  Congress and the several States shall have power
to enforce this article by appropriate legislation.

### 4. "Human Life" Statutes or Bills

Many human life statutes or bills have been proposed in Con-

gress.  The "Human Life Federalism" (S.J. Res. 110) bill pre-

sented by Senator Orrin G. Hatch (R-Utah) in 1981 has received

the most serious attention.  The bill has passed the Senate

Subcommittee on the Constitution and is expected to go before
the full Senate Judiciary Committee in 1982.


## B.   Funding Abortions


### 1.   Judicial Decisions


#### a.   *Beal v. Doe*, 432 U.S. 438 (1977)

The Court held that Title 19 of the Social Security Act
(Medicaid) did not require states to fund all abortions that
are legally permissible under state law; specifically, the state
may, as a matter of statutory construction, refuse to fund "unnecessary" though perhaps desirable medical services.


#### b.   *Maher v. Roe*, 432 U.S. 464 (1977)

This companion case involved a Connecticut Medicaid regulation that limited reimbursement to "medically necessary" abortions.  The regulation was challenged as a violation of equal
protection, since the state paid for childbirth, but not elective abortions.  The Supreme Court upheld the limitation on payments, stating that the regulation created no "barrier" to the
woman's exercise of her right that did not exist before the
regulation and that the regulation was "rationally related" to
the legitimate state interest in encouraging childbirth.  A
strong dissent by Justice Brennan argued that the effect of the

regulation violated equal protection because it "coerces poor

women to bear children they would not otherwise choose to

have. . ."

c.  *Poelker v. Doe*, 432 U.S. 519 (1977)

This decision held that public hospitals with obstetrical

units need not offer their services for elective abortion.

d.  *Harris v. McRae*,  448 U.S. 297 (1980)

The question before the court was whether the Hyde Amendment

by denying public funds for certain medically necessary abor-

tions contravenes the liberty or equal protection guarantees of

the Constitution.  The version of the Hyde Amendment under con-

sideration was:

> None of the funds provided by this joint resolution shall be
> used to perform abortions except where the life of the mother
> would be endangered if the fetus were carried to term; or except
> for such medical procedures necessary for the victims of rape or
> incest when such rape or incest has been reported promptly to a
> law enforcement agency or public health service.

Relying primarily on *Maher (supra)* the Court held that, since

the funding restriction created no obstacle to a woman exer-

cising her right to an abortion, it was permissible for the

state to encourage childbirth by funding it and not funding even

medically necessary abortions.  In the court's words (citing

*Maher*):  "although government may not place obstacles in the

path of a woman's exercise of her freedom of choice, it need not

remove those not of its own creation.  Indigency falls in the

latter category."  The logic of the case would permit the gov-

ernment to refuse to fund any abortions at all, even those designed to save the life of the pregnant woman.


2.  Congressional Actions

  a.  Hyde Amendment to the Departments of Labor and
      Health, Education, and Welfare Appropriations Act

The continuing history of the Hyde Amendments to the Departments of Labor and Health, Education, and Welfare Appropriations
bills is presented below:

  i.  Pub. L. 94-439 (1976)

The first Hyde Amendment prohibited the use of federal Medicaid funds for abortion, except in cases where the life of the
pregnant woman was endangered, during fiscal year (FY) 1977.
Despite President Ford's veto of the bill on September 29, 1976,
both houses overrode the veto on September 30, 1976, and the
bill became Pub. L. 94-439 on the same day.

  ii.  Pub. L. 95-205 (1977) and Pub. L. 95-480 (1978)

These new riders to the annual appropriations bills (for FY
1978 and FY 1979) allowed federal funding for abortions in cases
of promptly reported rape or incest and in cases where continuation of pregnancy would lead to long-lasting physical health
damage to the woman.  The provisions are as follows:

  *Provided*, That none of the funds provided for in this paragraph shall be used to perform abortions except where the life
  of the mother would be endangered if the fetus were carried to
  term; or except for such medical procedures necessary for the
  victims of rape or incest, when such rape or incest has been
  reported promptly to a law enforcement agency or public health

service; or except in those instances where severe and long-lasting physical health damage to the mother would result if the pregnancy were carried to term when so determined by two physicians.

Nor are payments prohibited for drugs or devices to prevent implantation of the fertilized ovum, or medical procedures necessary for the termination of an ectopic pregnancy.

The Secretary shall promptly issue regulations and establish procedures to ensure that the provisions of this section are rigorously enforced.

Sec. 210.  None of the funds provided for in this Act shall be used to perform abortions except where the life of the mother would be endangered if the fetus were carried to term; or except for such medical procedures necessary for the victims of rape or incest, when such rape or incest has been reported promptly to a law enforcement agency or public health service; or except in those instances where severe and long-lasting physical health damage to the mother would result if the pregnancy were carried to term when so determined by two physicians.

Nor are payments prohibited for drugs or devices to prevent implantation of the fertilized ovum, or for medical procedures necessary for the termination of an ectopic pregnancy.

### iii.  Pub. L. 96-123 (1979)

Congress reenacted the Hyde Amendment, but left out the previous exception made in cases of potential "serious and long-lasting health damages":

[N]one of the funds provided by this joint resolution shall be used to perform abortions except where the life of the mother would be endangered if the fetus were carried to term; or except for such medical procedures necessary for the victims of rape or incest when such rape or incest has been reported promptly to a law enforcement agency or public health service;

Nor are payments prohibited for drugs or devices to prevent implantation of the fertilized ovum, or for medical procedures necessary for the termination of an ectopic pregnancy.

### iv.  Public L. 96-369 (October 1, 1980)

This is the first of two Hyde Amendment bills to be passed in 1980 (it expired on December 15, 1980, and therefore required that another be passed before that date):

[N]one of the funds made available by this joint resolution
. . . shall be used to perform abortions except where the life
of the mother would be endangered if the fetus were carried to
term; or except for such medical procedures necessary for the
victims of rape or incest, when such rape has been reported
within seventy-two hours to a law enforcement agency or public
health service; nor are payments prohibited for drugs or devices to prevent implantation of the fertilized ovum, or for
medical procedures necessary for the termination of an ectopic
pregnancy: Provided, however, That the several states are and
shall remain free not to fund abortions to the extent that they
in their sole discretion deem appropriate.

### v.   Pub. L. 95-536 (December 16, 1980)

The following is the final Hyde Amendment bill to be passed

in 1980:

Sec. 109. . . . [N]one of the funds made available by this
joint resolution for programs and activities for. . . the
Departments of Labor, Health and Human Services and Education. . . shall be used to perform abortions except where the
life of the mother would be endangered if the fetus were carried to term; or except for such medical procedures necessary
for the victims of rape or incest, when such rape has within
seventy-two hours been reported to a law enforcement agency or
public health service; nor are payments prohibited for drugs or
devices to prevent implantation of the fertilized ovum, or for
medical procedures necessary for the termination of an ectopic
pregnancy. Provided, however, That the several States are and
shall remain free not to fund abortions to the extent that they
in their sole discretion deem appropriate.

### vi.   H.R. 3512 (May 21, 1981)

This bill struck down the exception made in previous Amend-

ments for victims of rape or incest.

### vii.   Pub. L. 97-92 (December 15, 1981)

The most recent continuing resolution allows Medicaid

funding only in cases were the woman's life is endangered.

This resolution became effective until March 31, 1982.

C.  Policy Statements on Abortion


1.  Church Policy Statements

Policy statements on abortion from 19 churches are summarized below (Source:   National Council of Churches, August
1978).


a.  American Baptist Churches

Abortion is a matter of responsible personal decision.
Urges that legislation be enacted to provide:

1.  That termination of pregnancy prior to end of 12th week
    be at request of individuals concerned and regarded as
    elective medical procedure governed by laws regulating
    medical practice and licensure.

2.  That after that period the abortion be performed only
    by duly licensed physicians in a regularly licensed
    hospital for one of the following reasons:

    a. Danger to physical or mental health of mother.

    b. Physical or mental defect of the fetus.

    c. Pregnancy due to rape, incest or other felonious
       acts.

       (Each of the three reasons to be supported by
       documented evidence; Convention, 1968.)

Opposition to constitutional amendment prohibiting abortion
(Baptist Joint Committee on Public Affairs, 1977).

b.  <u>American Lutheran Church</u>

Accepts possibility that an induced abortion may be a necessary option in individual human situations.  Each person needs
to be free to make this choice in the light of each individual
situation.  This statement has the status of "comment and
counsel"; General Convention, 1974.)

c.  <u>Christian Church (Disciples of Christ)</u>

Persons who must decide whether or not to undergo an abortion shall have the informed supportive resources of the Christian community to help them make responsible choices and the
full support of the congregation and individuals (General
Assembly, 1973).

Church respects differences in religious beliefs concerning
abortion and opposes, in accord with the principle of religious
liberty, any attempt to legislate a specific religious opinion
or belief concerning abortion upon all Americans (General
Assembly, 1975).

Church disapproved a resolution which "abhorred the wide-
spread practice of abortion" (General Assembly, 1975).

d.  <u>Church of the Brethren</u>

Brethren oppose abortion because it destroys fetal life.
Abortion should be accepted as an option only when all other
possible alternatives will lead to greater destruction of human
life, protection of freedom of moral choice, and availability of
good medical care (Annual Conference, 1972).

### e.  Episcopal Church

Termination of pregnancy is permissible in those cases where the physical or mental health of the mother is threatened seriously or where there is substantial reason to believe that the child would be badly deformed in mind or body, or where the pregnancy has resulted from rape or incest (General Convention, 1967; reaffirmed by General Convention of 1976).  Abortions for convenience are not a moral means of limitation for responsible birth control.  Church expresses unequivocal opposition to any national or state legislation which would abridge or deny the right of individuals to reach informed decisions in this matter and to act upon them (General Convention, 1976).

### f.  Greek Orthodox

Abortion is murder.  Orthodox condemn all procedures purporting to abort the embryo or fetus, whether by surgical or by chemical means.  The only time the Orthodox Church will reluctantly acquiesce to abortion is when the preponderance of medical opinion determines that unless the embryo or fetus is aborted, the mother will die (Official Statement from Chancery Office, 1978).

### g.  Lutheran Church in America

A woman or couple may decide responsibly to seek an abortion.  Earnest consideration should be given to the life and total health of the mother, her responsibilities in her family,

the state of development of the fetus, the economic and psychological stability of the home, the laws of the land, and the
consequences for society as a whole.  Church upholds its pastors
and other responsible counselors, and persons who conscien-
tiously make decisions about abortions (Convention, 1970).

### h.  Moravian Church, Northern Province

Decision to interrupt a pregnancy, consistent within time
limit recognized by the medical profession, is responsibility of
the individual(s) involved, based on their interpretation of
Christian teaching, with thought and with adequate medical and
spiritual counseling.  Abortions should be viewed in perspective
of bringing mercy to a difficult situation where other options
may be more destructive.  Abortion should not be used as a means
of population control (Synod of 1970).

### i.  Orthodox Church in America

Willful aborting of unborn children, as an act of murder, is
contrary to the will of God.  The Church recognizes the existence of certain extreme cases in which difficult moral decisions must be made in view of saving human life and fully
sympathizes with those who must make such decisions.  Whatever
the decisions of courts and human legislatures, the Church cannot accept the willful destruction of an unborn child at any
stage of its development as anything other than the destruction
of life (Encyclical Letter of the Holy Synod of Bishop 1976).

An abortion for convenience, at any stage of gestation, is a
violent termination of life and therefore is contrary to the
teaching of the Orthodox Church (Most Reverend Metropolitan
Ireney, 1973).

### j.  Presbyterian Church in Canada

Morally indefensible to legalize abortion in order to reduce
the number of illegal abortions or as a method of population
control.  However, as the mother's life and indeed physical and
mental health of the mother are more important than the life of
the fetus, when these are seriously threatened, abortion is not
precluded (General Assembly, 1967; reaffirmed in 1972).  Inter-
pretations of "life" and "health" must be strict (General
Assembly, 1976).

### k.  Presbyterian Church in the United States

Decision to terminate a pregnancy should never be made
lightly or in haste.  Willful termination of a pregnancy by medical means on considered decision of a pregnant woman may on
occasion be morally justifiable.  Possible justifying circumstances: medical indications of physical or mental deformity,
conception as a result of rape or incest, physical or mental
health of either mother or child gravely threatened, socio-
economic condition of the family (General Assembly, 1970).

1. Reformed Church in America

Reaffirmed General Synod statement of 1973 that abortion
ought not to be practiced at all, but in a complex society where
one form of evil is often pitted against another form of evil
there can be exceptions. Abortions for convenience ought not to
be permitted. No person should be forced or encouraged to undergo or to participate in an abortion when it is against the person's moral beliefs. Christian community should play supportive
role for those making a decision about abortion, should make
known alternatives to abortion. All who counsel those with
problem pregnancies are urged to uphold alternatives to abortion. Members are called upon to support efforts for constitutional changes to provide legal protection for the unborn (General Synod, 1975).

m. Roman Catholic Church

The direct interruption of the generative process already
begun, and above all, directly willed and procured abortion,
even if for therapeutic reasons, are to be absolutely excluded
as licit means of regulating birth. It is not licit, even for
the gravest reasons, to do evil so that good may follow therefrom, even when the intention is to safeguard or promote individual, family, or social well-being (Humanae Vitae, Encyclical
Letter of Paul VI, 1968).

### n.  Southern Baptist Convention

Call to Southern Baptists and all citizens of the nation to work to change those attitudes and conditions which encourage many people to turn to abortion as a means of birth control. Affirm conviction about limited role of government in dealing with matters relating to abortion, and support right of expectant mothers to full range of medical services and personal counseling for preservation of life and health (General Convention, 1977).

### o.  Syrian Orthodox Church of Antioch

Life is sacred and God-given.  Only in cases where the mother's continued pregnancy would mean her death is a clinical abortion permitted.  If both mother and child can be saved, abortion may not be performed (Letter of Archbishop Athanasius Y. Samuel, 1973).

### p.  United Church of Canada

Abortion not approved either as means of limiting or spacing one's family or as relief to an ummarried mother, because it involves destruction of a human life.  However, if in judgment of reputable medical authorities, the continuation of a pregnancy seriously endangers the physical or mental health of the mother, therapeutic abortion may be necessary (General Council, 1960).

### q.  United Church of Christ

Calls for repeal of all legal prohibitions of physician-
performed abortions, thus making voluntary and medically safe
abortions legally available to all women.  Asks that adequate
protection be given to "conscientious objectors" against abortion, including physicians, nurses, and prospective mothers
(General Synod, 1974).

### r.  United Methodist Church

Church recognized tragic conflicts of unborn life with
mother's life and well-being that may warrant abortion and
therefore supports legal options of abortion under proper medical procedures.  Since more guidance is needed than governmental laws and regulations, decision about abortion should be made
after thorough and thoughtful consideration by parties involved,
with medical and pastoral counsel (Social Principles Section,
Book of Discipline of the United Methodist Church, 1976).

### s.  United Presbyterian Church in the United States of America

Women should have full freedom of personal choice concerning
completion or termination of their pregnancies.  Abortion should
not be restricted by law except that it be performed under the
direction and control of a properly licensed physician.  Supports establishment of medically sound, easily available, low-
cost abortion services (General Assembly, 1972).

2.  Declaration of Oslo (1970)

The "Statement on Therapeutic Abortion" adopted by the 24th

World Medical Assembly, Oslo, Norway, 1970 is reprinted below:

1.  The first moral principle imposed upon the doctor is
respect for human life as expressed in a clause of the Declaration of Geneva:  "I will maintain the utmost respect for human
life from the time of conception."
2.  Circumstances which bring the vital interests of a
mother into conflict with the vital interests of her unborn
child create a dilemma and raise the question whether or not
the pregnancy should be deliberately terminated.
3.  Diversity of response to this situation results from
the diversity of attitudes towards the life of the unborn child.
This is a matter of individual conviction and conscience which
must be respected.
4.  It is not the role of the medical profession to determine the attitudes and rules of any particular state or community in this matter, but it is our duty to attempt both to
ensure the protection of our patients and to safeguard the
rights of the doctor within society.
5.  Therefore, where the law allows therapeutic abortion to
be performed, or legislation to that effect is contemplated,
and this is not against the policy of the national medical association, and where the legislature desires or will accept the
guidance of the medical profession, the following principles are
approved:
   a) Abortion should be performed only as a therapeutic
      measure.
   b) A decision to terminate pregnancy normally should be
      approved in writing by at least two doctors chosen for      1
      their professional competence.
   c) The procedure should be performed by a doctor competent
      to do so in premises approved by the appropriate author-
      ity.
6. If the doctor considers that his convictions do not allow
him to advise or perform an abortion, he may withdraw while
ensuring the continuity of (medical) care by a qualified col-
league.
7.  This statement, while it is endorsed by the General
Assembly of the World Medical Association, is not to be
regarded as binding on any individual member association unless
it is adopted by that member association.

D.  Prenatal Procedures

1.  Fetal Research

a.  Federal Guidelines

i.  45 CFR Part 46:  Protection of Human Subjects:
    Fetuses, Pregnant Women, and In Vitro Fertil-
    ization (1975)

This amendment (40 *Federal Register* 33526) to 45 CFR Part 46

was a response to recommendations submitted by the National Com-

mission for the Protection of Human Subjects of Biomedical and

Behavioral Research on May 21, 1975.  In addition to lifting a

moratorium on fetal research that had been imposed by the De-

partment of Health, Education, and Welfare (HEW) on August 27,

1974 (39 FR 30962), this document proposed guidelines for re-

search involving fetuses, pregnant women, and human in vitro

fertilization.  These regulations follow:

Subpart B--Additional Protections Pertaining to Research,
    Development, and Related Activities Involving Fetuses, Preg-
    nant Women, and Human in Vitro Fertilization.

§ 46.201 Applicability.

(a) The regulations in this subpart are applicable to all
Department of Health, Education, and Welfare grants and con-
tracts supporting research, development, and related activities
involving: (1) The fetus, (2) pregnant women, and (3) human *in
vitro* fertilization.
(b) Nothing in this subpart shall be construed as indicating
that compliance with the procedures set forth herein will in any
way render inapplicable pertinent State or local laws bearing
upon activities covered by this subpart.
(c) The requirements of this subpart are in addition to
those imposed under the other subparts of this part.

§ 46.202  Purpose.

It is the purpose of this subpart to provide additional safeguards in reviewing activities to which this subpart is applicable to assure that they conform to appropriate ethical standards and relate to important societal needs.

§ 46.203  Definitions.

As used in this subpart:

(a) "Secretary" means the Secretary of Health, Education, and Welfare and any other officer or employee of the Department of Health, Education, and Welfare to whom authority has been delegated.

(b) "Pregnancy" encompasses the period of time from confirmation of implantation until expulsion or extraction of the fetus.

(c) "Fetus" means the product of conception from the time of implantation until a determination is made, following expulsion or extraction of the fetus, that it is viable.

(d) "Viable" as it pertains to the fetus means being able, after either spontaneous or induced delivery, to survive (given the benefit of available medical therapy) to the point of independently maintaining heart beat and respiration. The Secretary may from time to time, taking into account medical advances, publish in the Federal Register guidelines to assist in determining whether a fetus is viable for purposes of this subpart. If a fetus is viable after delivery, it is a premature infant.

(e) "Nonviable fetus" means a fetus *ex utero* which, although living, is not viable.

(f) "Dead fetus" means a fetus *ex utero* which exhibits neither heartbeat, spontaneous respiratory activity, spontaneous movement of voluntary muscles, nor pulsation of the umbilical cord (if still attached).

(g) "*In vitro* fertilization" means any fertilization of human ova which occurs outside the body of a female, either through admixture of donor human sperm and ova or by any other means.

§ 46.204  Ethical Advisory Board.

(a) Two Ethical Advisory Boards shall be established by the Secretary. Members of these Boards shall be so selected that the Boards will be competent to deal with medical, legal, social, ethical, and related issues and may include, for example, research scientists, physicians, psychologists, sociologists, educators, lawyers, and ethicists, as well as representatives of the general public. No board member may be a regular, full-time employee of the Federal Government.

(b) One Board shall be advisory to the Public Health Service and its components.  One Board shall be advisory to all other agencies and components within the Department of Health, Education, and Welfare.

(c) At the request of the Secretary, the appropriate Ethical Advisory Board shall render advice consistent with the policies and requirements of this Part as to ethical issues, involving activities covered by this subpart, raised by individual applications or proposals.  In addition, upon request by the Secretary, the appropriate Board shall render advice as to classes of applications or proposals and general policies, guidelines and procedures.

(d) A Board may establish, with the approval of the Secretary, classes of applications or proposals which:  (1) Must be submitted to the Board, or (2) need not be submitted to the Board.  Where the Board so establishes a class of applications of proposals which must be submitted, no application or proposal within the class may be funded by the Department or any component thereof until the application or proposal has been reviewed by the Board and the Board has rendered advice as to its acceptability from an ethical standpoint.

(e) No application or proposal involving human *in vitro* fertilization may be funded by the Department or any component thereof until the application or proposal has been reviewed by the Ethical Advisory Board and the Board has rendered advice as to its acceptability from an ethical standpoint.

§ 46.205  Additional duties of the Institutional Review Boards in connection with activities involving fetuses, pregnant women, or human in vitro fertilization.

(a) In addition to the responsibilities prescribed for Institutional Review Boards under Subpart A of this part, the applicant's or offeror's Board shall with respect to activities covered by this subpart, carry out the following additional duties:

(1) Determine that all aspects of the activity meet the requirements of this subpart;

(2) Determine that adequate consideration has been given to the manner in which potential subjects will be selected, and adequate provision has been made by the applicant or offeror for monitoring the actual informed consent process (e.g., through such mechanisms, when appropriate, as participation by the Institutional Review Board or subject advocates in:
(i) Overseeing the actual process by which individual consents required by this subpart are secured either by approving induction of each individual into the activity or verifying, perhaps through sampling, that approved procedures for induction of individuals into the activity are being followed, and (ii) monitoring the progress of the activity and intervening as

necessary through such steps as visits to the activity site
and continuing evaluation to determine if any unanticipated
risks have arisen):

(3) Carry out such other responsibilities as may be assigned
by the Secretary.

(b) No award may be issued until the applicant or offeror
has certified to the Secretary that the Institutional Review
Board has made the determinations required under paragraph (a)
of this section and the Secretary has approved these determinations, as provided in § 46.115 of Subpart A of this part.

(c) Applicants or offerors seeking support for activities
covered by this subpart must provide for the designation of an
Institutional Review Board, subject to approval by the Secretary, where no such Board has been established under Subpart A
of this part.

## § 46.206  General limitations

(a) No activity to which this subpart is applicable may be
undertaken unless:

(1) Appropriate studies on animals and nonpregnant individuals have been completed;

(2) Except where the purpose of the activity is to meet the
health needs of the particular fetus, the risk to the fetis is
minimal and, in all cases, is the least possible risk for
achieving the objectives of the activity;

(3) Individuals engaged in the activity will have no part
in:  (i) any decisions as to the timing, method, and procedures
used to terminate the pregnancy, and (ii) determining the viability of the fetus at the termination of the pregnancy; and

(4)  No procedural changes which may cause greater than
minimal risk to the fetus or the pregnant woman will be intro-
duced into the procedure for terminating the pregnancy solely
in the interest of the activity.

(b) No inducements, monetary or otherwise, may be offered
to terminate pregnancy for purposes of the activity.

## § 406.207  Activities directed toward pregnant women as subjects

(a) No pregnant woman may be involved as a subject in an
activity covered by this subpart unless: (1) The purpose of the
activity is to meet the health needs of the mother and the fetus
will be placed at risk only to the minimum extent necessary to
meet such needs, or (2) the risk to the fetus is minimal.

(b) An activity permitted under paragraph (a) of this section may be conducted only if the mother and father are legally
competent and have given their informed consent after having
been fully informed regarding possible impact on the fetus,
except that the father's informed consent need not be secured
if:  (1) The purpose of the activity is to meet the health needs

of the mother; (2) his identity or whereabouts cannot reasonably be ascertained; (3) he is not reasonably available; or (4) the pregnancy resulted from rape.

§ 46.208  Activities directed toward fetuses in utero as
    subjects.

(a) No fetus *in utero* may be involved as a subject in any activity covered by this subpart unless:  (1) The purpose of the activity is to meet the health needs of the particular fetus and the fetus will be placed at risk only to the minimum extent necessary to meet such needs, or (2) the risk to the fetus imposed by the research is minimal and the purpose of the activity is the development of important biomedical knowledge which cannot be obtained by other means.

(b) An activity permitted under paragraph (a) of this section may be conducted only if the mother and father are legally competent and have given their informed consent, except that the father's consent need not be secured if:  (1) His identity or whereabouts cannot reasonably be ascertained, (2) he is not reasonably available, or (3) the pregnancy resulted from rape.

§ 46.209  Activities directed toward fetuses ex utero, including
    nonviable fetuses, as subjects.

(a) No fetus *ex utero* may be involved as a subject in an activity covered by this subpart until it has been ascertained whether the particular fetus is viable, unless: (1) There will be no added risk to the fetus resulting from the activity, and (2) the purpose of the activity is the development of important biomedical knowledge which cannot be obtained by other means.

(b) no nonviable fetus may be involved as a subject in an activity covered by this subpart unless:  (1) Vital functions of the fetus will not be artificially maintained except where the purpose of the activity is to develop new methods for enabling fetuses to survive to the point of viability, (2) experimental activities which of themselves would terminate the heartbeat or respiration of the fetus will not be employed, and (3) the purpose of the activity is the development of important biomedical knowledge which cannot be obtained by other means.

(c) In the event the fetus *ex utero* is found to be viable, it may be included as a subject in the activity only to the extent permitted by and in accordance with the requirements of other subparts of this part.

(d) An activity permitted under paragraph (a) or (b) of this section may be conducted only if the mother and father are legally competent and have given their informed consent, except that the father's informed consent need not be secured if: (1) his identity or whereabouts cannot reasonably be ascertained, (2) he is not reasonably available, or (3) the pregnancy resulted from rape.

§ 46.210  Activities involving the dead fetus, fetal material,
or the placenta.

Activities involving the dead fetus, mascerated fetal material, or cells, tissue, or organs excised from a dead fetus
shall be conducted only in accordance with any applicable State
or local laws regarding such activities.

§ 46.211  Modification or waiver of specific requirements.

Upon the request of an applicant or offeror (with the approval of its Institutional Review Board), the Secretary may
modify or waive specific requirements of this subpart, with the
approval of the Ethical Advisory Board after such opportunity
for public comment as the Ethical Advisory Board considers
appropriate in the particular instance.  In making such decisions, the Secretary will consider whether the risks to the
subject are so outweighed by the sum of the benefit to the
subject and the importance of the knowledge to be gained as to
warrant such modification or waiver and that such benefits cannot be gained except through a modification or waiver.  Any
such modifications or waivers will be published as notices in
the Federal Register.

Subpart C--General Provisions

§ 46.301  Activities conducted by Department employees.

The regulations of this part are applicable as well to all
research, development, and related activities conducted by employees of the Department of Health, Education, and Welfare,
except that each Principal Operating Component head may adopt
such non-substantive procedural modifications as may be appropriate from an administrative standpoint.

On July 29, 1975, the Office of the Secretary of the Depart-

ment of Health, Education, and Welfare published in the Federal

Register (40 FR 33552) further guidelines for determining the

viability of a fetus, including in the definition of viability

"an estimated gestational age of 20 weeks or more and a body

weight of 500 grams or more."

b.  Recommendations of the Ethics Advisory Board (HEW)
    on Research Involving Human *In Vitro* Fertilization
    and Embryo Transfer, May 4, 1979

Conclusion (1) The Department should consider support of
carefully designed research involving *in vitro* fertilization and
embryo transfer in animals, including nonhuman primates, in
order to obtain a better understanding of the process of fertilization, implantation and embryo development, to assess the
risks to both mother and offspring associated with such procedures, and to improve the efficacy of the procedure
Conclusion (2) The Ethics Advisory Board finds that it is
acceptable from an ethical standpoint to undertake research
involving human *in vitro* fertilization and embryo transfer provided that:
   A.  If the research involves human *in vitro* fertilization
       without embryo transfer, the following conditions are
       satisfied:
       1.  The research complies with all appropriate provi-
           visions of the regulations governing research with
           human subjects (45 CFR 46);
       2.  The research is designed primarily:  (A) To estab-
           lish the safety and efficacy of embryo transfer and
           (B) to obtain important scientific information
           toward that end not reasonably attainable by other
           means;
       3.  Human gametes used in such research will be obtained
           exclusively from persons who have been informed of
           the nature and purpose of the research in which such
           materials will be used and have specifically con-
           sented to such use;
       4.  No embryos will be sustained *in vitro* beyond the
           stage normally associated with the completion of
           implantation (14 days after fertilization); and
       5.  All interested parties and the general public will
           be advised if evidence begins to show that the pro-
           cedure entails risks of abnormal offspring higher
           than those associated with natural human reproduc-
           tion.
   B.  In addition, if the research involves embryo transfer
       following human *in vitro* fertilization, embryo transfer
       will be attempted only with gametes obtained from law-
       fully married couples.
Conclusion (3) The Board finds it acceptable from an ethical
standpoint for the department to support or conduct research
involving human *in vitro* fertilization and embryo transfer,
provided that the applicable conditions set forth in conclusion
(2) are met.  However, the board has decided not to address the
question of the level of funding, if any, which such research
might be given.

Conclusion (4) The National Institute of Child Health and
Human Development (NICHD) and other appropriate agencies should
work with professional societies, foreign governments and international organizations to collect, analyze and disseminate information derived from research (in both animals and humans) and
clinical experience throughout the world involving *in vitro* fertilization and embryo transfer.

Conclusion (5) The Secretary should encourage the development of a uniform or model law to clarify the legal status of
children born as a result of *in vitro* fertilization and embryo
transfer.  To the extent that funds may be necessary to develop
such legislation, the Department should consider providing
appropriate support.


c.  Selected State Statutes on Fetal Research

At least 16 states passed statutes designed to outlaw or

limit research on fetuses in the wake of *Roe v. Wade*.  The

states were California, Illinois, Indiana, Kentucky, Louisiana,

Maine, Massachusetts, Missouri, North Dakota, Ohio, Pennsyl-

vania, South Dakota, Minnesota, Montana, Nebraska and Utah.  The

following are some examples:

i.  Louisiana Rev. Stat. Ann. sec. 14:87.2
    (West, 1974)

Human experimentation is the use of any live born human
being, without consent of that live born human being, as hereinafter defined, for any scientific or laboratory research or
any kind of experimentation or study except to protect or preserve the life and health of said live born human being, or the
conduct, on a human embryo or fetus in utero, of any experimentation or study except to preserve the life or to improve the
health of said human embryo or fetus.

A human being is live born, or there is a live birth, whenever there is the complete expulsion or extraction from its
mother of a human embryo or fetus, irrespective of the duration
of pregnancy, which after such separation, breathes or shows any
other evidence of life such as beating of the heart, pulsation
of the umbilical cord, or movement of voluntary muscles, whether
or not the umbilical cord has been cut or the placenta is attached.

Whoever commits the crime of human experimentation shall be imprisoned at hard labor for not less than five nor more than twenty years, or fined not more than ten thousand dollars, or both.

### ii.    Kentucky Rev. Stat. Ann. sec. 436.026
### (Cum. Supp. 1974)

Whoever shall sell, transfer, distribute or give away any live or viable aborted child or permits such child to be used for any form of experimentation shall be imprisoned in the penitentiary for a term of not less than ten (10) nor more than twenty (20) years.  Nothing contained in this section shall be construed as prohibiting adoption or foster care proeedings pursuant to the provisions of the laws of the commonwealth.

### iii.   California Health & Safety Code Ann.
### sec. 25957 (1973)

(a) Except as provided in subdivision (b) at the conclusion of any scientific or laboratory research or any other kind of experimentation or study upon fetal remains, such fetal remains shall be promptly interred or disposed of by incineration.
Storage of such fetal remains prior to the completion of the research, experimentation, or study shall be in a place not open to the public, and the method of storage shall prevent any deterioration of the fetal remains which would create a health hazard.
(b) The provisions of subdivision (a) shall not apply to public or private educational institutions.
Any violation of this section is a misdemeanor.

### iv.    Indiana Code sec. 10-112 (Supp. 1977)

No experiments except pathological examinations may be conducted on any fetus aborted under this chapter, nor may any fetus so aborted be transported out of this state for experimental purposes.  A person who conducts such an experiment or so transports such a fetus commits a class A misdemeanor.

2.  Caesarean Sections

   a.  Judicial Decisions

      i. *Jefferson v. Griffin Spalding City Hospital,*
         274 S.E. 2nd 457 (Ga. 1981)

On Friday, January 23, the Georgia Department of Human Resources, acting through the Butts County Department of Family
and Children Services, petitioned the Juvenile Court of Butts
County for temporary custody of the unborn child, alleging that
the child was a deprived child without proper parental care necessary for his or her physical health (see Code Ann. § 24A-401
(h)(1)), and praying for an order requiring the mother to submit
to a caesarean section.  After appointing counsel for the parents and for the child, the court conducted a joint hearing in
both the superior court and juvenile court cases and entered
the following order on the afternoon of January 23:

   "This action in the Superior Court of Butts County was
heard and decided yesterday, January 22, 1981.
   "Based on the evidence presented, the Court finds that
Jessie Mae Jefferson is due to begin labor at any moment.
There is a 99 to 100 percent certainty that the unborn
child will die if she attempts to have the child by vaginal
delivery.  There is a 99 to 100 percent chance that the
child will live if the baby is delivered by Caesarean section prior to the beginning of labor.  There is a 50 percent chance that Mrs. Jefferson herself will die if vaginal
delivery is attempted.  There is an almost 100 percent
chance that Mrs. Jefferson will survive if a delivery by
Caesarean section is done prior to the beginning of labor.
The Court finds that as a matter of fact the child is a
human being fully capable of sustaining life independent
of the mother.
   "Mrs. Jefferson and her husband have refused and continue to refuse to give consent to a Caesarean section.
This refusal is based entirely on the religious beliefs of
Mr. and Mrs. Jefferson.  They are of the view that the Lord
has healed her body and that whatever happens to the child
will be the Lord's will.
   "Based on these findings, the Court concludes and finds
as a matter of law that this child is a viable human being
and entitled to the protection of the Juvenile Court Code
of Georgia.  The Court concludes that this child is without
the proper parental care and subsistence necessary for his
or her physical life and health.
   "Temporary custody of the unborn child is hereby
granted to the State of Georgia Department of Human

Resources and the Butts County Department of Family and
Children Services.  The Department shall have full authority
to make all decisions, including giving consent to the surgical delivery appertaining to the birth of this child.  The
temporary custody of the Department shall terminate when the
child has been successfully brought from its mother's body
into the world or until the child dies, whichever shall
happen.

"Because of the unique nature of these cases, the
powers of the Superior Court of Butts County are invoked
and the defendant, Jessie Mae Jefferson, is hereby Ordered
to submit to a sonogram (ultrasound) at the Griffin Spalding
County Hospital or some other place which may be chosen by
her where such procedure can be given.  Should said sonogram
indicate to the attending physician that the complete placenta privia is still blocking the child's passage into this
world, Jessie Mae Jefferson, is Ordered to submit to a Caesarean section and related procedures considered necessary
by the attending physician to sustain the life of this
child.

"The Court finds that the State has an interest in the
life of this unborn, living human being.  The Court finds
that the intrusion involved into the life of Jessie Mae Jefferson and her husband, John W. Jefferson, is outweighed by
the duty of the State to protect a living, unborn human
being from meeting his or her death before being given the
opportunity to live.

"This Order shall be effective at 10:00 a.m. on Satur-
day, January 24, 1981, unless a stay is granted by the Supreme Court of Georgia or some other Court having the authority to stay an Order of this Court."

The parents filed their motion for stay in this court at
about 5:30 p.m. on January 23 and after hearing oral argument
from the attorneys for the parents, the child, the Department of
Human Resources and the Butts County Department of Family and
Children's Services, and after considering additional authorities located by our law assistants, this court entered the
following order on the evening of January 23:

"It is ordered that the Motion for Stay filed in this
matter is hereby denied.  The trial court's orders are
effective immediately.  *Roe v. Wade*, 410 U.S. 113 (1973);
*Raleigh Fitkin-Paul Morgan Memorial Hospital v. Anderson* 42
N.J. 421 (1964); *Strunk v. Strunk*, Ky., 445 S.W. 2d 145
(1969)."

MOTION FOR STAY DENIED.

## II.  EUTHANASIA AND THE RIGHT TO REFUSE TREATMENT

## A.  Judicial Decisions

### 1.  *Matter of Quinlan*, 355 A.2d 647, 70 N.J. 10 (1976)

The central figure in this tragic case is Karen Ann Quinlan, a New Jersey resident.  At the age of 22, she lies in a debilitated and allegedly moribund state at Saint Clare's Hospital in Denville, New Jersey.  The litigation has to do, in final analysis, with her life,--its continuance or cessation,--and the responsibilities, rights and duties, with regard to any fateful decision concerning it, of her family, her guardian, her doctors, the hospital, the State through its law enforcement authorities, and finally the courts of justice.

It is the issue of the constitutional right of privacy that has given us most concern, in the exceptional circumstances of this case.  Here a loving parent, *qua* parent and raising the rights of his incompetent and profoundly damaged daughter, probably irreversibly doomed to no more than a biologically vegetative remnant of life, is before the court.  He seeks authorization to abandon specialized technological procedures which can only maintain for a time a body having no potential for resumption or continuance of other than a "vegetative" existence.

We have no doubt, in these unhappy circumstances, that if Karen were herself miraculously lucid for an interval (not altering the existing prognosis of the condition to which she would soon return) and perceptive of her irreversible condition, she could effectively decide upon discontinuance of the life-support apparatus, even if it meant the prospect of natural death.  To this extent we may distinguish *Hester, supra,* which concerned a severely injured young woman (Delores Heston), whose life depended on surgery and blood transfusion; and who was in such extreme shock that she was unable to express an informed choice (although the Court apparently considered the case as if the patient's own religious decision to resist transfusion were at stake); but most importantly a patient apparently salvable to long life and vibrant health;--a situation not at all like the present case.

51

We have no hesitancy in deciding, in the instant diametrical-
ly opposite case, that no external compelling interest of the
State could compel Karen to endure the unendurable, only to veg-
etate a few measurable months with no realistic possibility of
returning to any semblance of cognitive or sapient life. We
perceive no thread of logic distinguishing between such a choice
on Karen's part and a similar choice which, under the evidence
in this case, could be made by a competent patient terminally
ill, riddled by cancer and suffering great pain; such a patient
would not be resuscitated or put on a respirator in the example
described by Dr. Korein, and *a fortiori* would not be kept *against
his will* on a respirator.

Although the Constitution does not explicitly mention a
right of privacy, Supreme Court decisions have recognized that
a right of personal privacy exists and that certain areas of
privacy are guaranteed under the Constitution. . . . The Court
has interdicted judicial intrusion into many aspects of personal
decision, sometimes basing this restraint upon the conception of
a limitation of judicial interest and responsibility, such as
with regard to contraception and its relationship to family life
and decision. *Griswold v. Connecticut,* 381 U.S. 479, (1965).

The Court in *Griswold* found the unwritten constitutional
right of privacy to exist in the penumbra of specific guarantees
of the Bill of Rights "formed by emanations from those guarantees that help give them life and substance." 381 U.S. at 484.
Presumably this right is broad enough to encompass a patient's
decision to decline medical treatment under certain circumstances, in much the same way as it is broad enough to encompass
a woman's decision to terminate pregnancy under certain conditions. *Roe v. Wade,* 410 U.S. 113 (1973).

The claimed interests of the State in this case are essentially the preservation and sanctity of human life and defense
of the right of the physician to administer medical treatment
according to his best judgment. In this case the doctors say
that removing Karen from the respirator will conflict with their
professional judgment. The plantiff answers that Karen's present treatment serves only a maintenance function; that the respirator cannot cure or improve her condition but at best can
only prolong her inevitable slow deterioration and death; and
that the interests of the patient, as seen by her surrogate, the
guardian, must be evaluated by the court as predominant, even
in the face of an opinion *contra* by the present attending physicians. Plaintiff's distinction is significant. The nature
of Karen's care and the realistic chances of her recovery are
quite unlike those of the patients discussed in many of the
cases where treatments were ordered. In many of those cases
the medical procedure required (usually a transfusion) constituted a minimal bodily invasion and the chances of recovery and

return to functioning life were very good. We think that the
State's interest *contra* weakens and the individual's right to
privacy grows as the degree of bodily invasion increases and the
prognosis dims. Ultimately there comes a point at which the individual's rights overcome the State interest. It is for that
reason that we believe Karen's choice, if she were competent to
make it, would be vindicated by the law. Her prognosis is extremely poor,--she will never resume cognitive life. And the
bodily invasion is very great,--she requires 24 hour intensive
nursing care, antibiotics, the assistance of a respirator, a
catheter and feeding tube.

Our affirmation of Karen's independent right of choice, however, would ordinarily be based upon her competency to assert
it. The sad truth, however, is that she is grossly incompetent
and we cannot discern her supposed choice based on the testimony
of her previous conversations with friends, where such testimony is without sufficient probative weight. 137 N.J. Super at
260, 348, A.2d 801. Nevertheless we have concluded that Karen's
right of privacy may be asserted on her behalf by her guardian
under the peculiar circumstances here present.

If a putative decision by Karen to permit this non-cogni-
tive, vegetative existence to terminate by natural forces is
regarded as a valuable incident of her right of privacy, as we
believe it to be, then it should not be discarded solely on the
basis that her condition prevents her conscious exercise of the
choice. The only practical way to prevent destruction of the
right is to permit the guardian and family of Karen to render
their best judgment, subject to the qualifications hereinafter
stated, as to whether she would exercise it in these circumstances. If their conclusion is in the affirmative this decision should be accepted by a society the overwhelming majority
of whose members would, we think, in similar circumstances, exercise such a choice in the same way for themselves or for those
closest to them. It is for this reason that we determine that
Karen's right of privacy may be asserted in her behalf, in this
respect, by her guardian and family under the particular circumstances presented by this record.

[T]here must be a way to free physicians, in the pursuit of
their healing vocation, from possible contamination by self-
interest or self-protection concerns which would inhibit their
independent medical judgments for the well-being of their dying
patients. We would hope that this opinion might be serviceable
to some degree in ameliorating the professional problems under
discussion.

A technique  aimed at the underlying difficulty (though in
a somewhat broader context) is described by Dr. Karen Teel, a
pediatrician and a director of Pediatric Education, who writes
in the *Baylor Law Review* under the title "The Physician's Di-

lemma: A Doctor's View: What The Law Should Be." Dr. Teel re-
calls:

> Physicians, by virtue of their responsibility for med-
> cal judgments are, partly by choice and partly by default,
> charged with the responsibility of making ethical judgments
> which we are sometimes ill-equipped to make. We are not al-
> ways morally and legally authorized to make them. The phy-
> sician is thereby assuming a civil and criminal liability
> that, as often as not, he does not even realize as a factor
> in his decision.

> I suggest that it would be more appropriate to provide a
> regular forum for more input and dialogue in individual situa-
> tions and to allow the responsibility of these judgments to be
> shared. Many hospitals have established an Ethics Committee
> composed of physicians, social workers, attorneys, and theologi-
> ans, * * * which serves to review the individual circumstances
> of ethical dilemma and which has provided much in the way of
> assistance and safeguards for patients and their medical care-
> takers. Generally, the authority of these committees is pri-
> marily restricted to the hospital setting and their official
> status is more that of an advisory body than of an enforcing
> body.
>   The concept of an Ethics Committee which has this kind of
> organization and is readily accessible to those persons render-
> ing medical care to patients, would be, I think, the most prom-
> ising direction for further study at this point. * * *
>   The trial court was apparently convinced of the high char-
> acter of Joseph Quinlan and his general suitability as guardian
> under other circumstances, describing him as "very sincere,
> moral, ethical and religious." The court felt, however, that
> the obligation to concur in the medical care and treatment of
> his daughter would be a source of anguish to him and would dis-
> tort his "decision-making processes." We disagree, for we
> sense from the whole record before us that while Mr. Quinlan
> feels a natural grief, and understandably sorrows because of
> the tragedy which has befallen his daughter, his strength of
> purpose and character far outweighs these sentiments and quali-
> fies him eminently for guardianship of the person as well as
> the property of his daughter. Hence we discern no valid reason
> to overrule the statutory intendment of preference to the next
> of kin.

> We thus arrive at the formulation of the declaratory re-
> lief which we have concluded is appropriate to this case. Some
> time has passed since Karen's physical and mental condition was
> described to the Court. At that time her continuing deteriora-

tion was plainly projected.  Since the record has not been expanded we assume that she is now even more fragile and nearer to death than she was then.  Since her present treating physicians may give reconsideration to her present posture in the light of this opinion, and since we are transferring to the plaintiff as guardian the choice of the attending physician and therefore other physicians may be in charge of the case who may take a different view from that of the present attending physicians, we herewith declare the following affirmative relief on behalf of the plaintiff.  Upon the concurrence of the guardian and family of Karen, should the responsible attending physicians conclude that there is no reasonable possibility of Karen's ever emerging from her present comatose condition to a cognitive, sapient state and that the life-support apparatus now being administered to Karen should be discontinued, they shall consult with the hospital "Ethics Committee" or like body of the institution in which Karen is then hospitalized.  If that consultative body agrees that there is no reasonable possibility of Karen's ever emerging from her present comatose condition to a cognitive, sapient state, the present life-support system may be withdrawn and said action shall be without any civil or criminal liability therefor on the part of any participant, whether guardian, physician, hospital or others.  We herewith specifically so hold.

We therefore remand this record to the trial court to implement (without further testimonial hearing) the following decisions:

1. To discharge, with the thanks of the Court for his service, the present guardian of the person of Karen Quinlan, Thomas R. Curtin, Esquire, a member of the Bar and an officer of the court.
2. To appoint Joseph Quinlan as guardian of the person of Karen Quinlan with full power to make decisions with regard to the identity of her treating physicians.

We repeat for the sake of emphasis and clarity that upon the concurrence of the guardian and family of Karen, should the responsible attending physicians conclude that there is no reasonable possibility of Karen's ever emerging from her present comatose condition to a cognitive, sapient state and that the life-support apparatus now being administered to Karen should be discontinued, they shall consult with the hospital "Ethics Committee" or like body of the institution in which Karen is then hospitalized.  If that consultative body agrees that there is no reasonable possibility of Karen's ever emerging from her present comatose condition to a cognitive sapient state, the

present life-support system may be withdrawn and said action
shall be without any civil or criminal liability therefor on
the part of any participant, whether guardian, physician, hospital or others.

By the above ruling we do not intend to be understood as im-
plying that a proceeding for judicial declaratory relief is necessarily required for the implementation of comparable decisions
in the field of medical practice.

2.  Competent Patients

a. *Erickson v. Dilgard*, 44 Misc. 2d 27, 252 N.Y.S.2d
   705 (Sup. Ct. 1962)

Jacob Delgard, Sr., was suffering from upper-gastro-

intestinal bleeding; his physicians recommended an operation

and blood transfusion.  He refused to submit to the operation

unless the doctors assured him there would be no blood trans-

fusion.  The doctors refused and the court upheld the patient's

decision even though his physician thought it might lead to his

death:  " . . . it is the individual who is the subject of a

medical decision who has the final say and this must necessar-

ily be so in a system of government which gives the greatest

possible protection to the individual in the furtherance of his

own desires."

b. *Lane v. Candura*, 376 N.E.2d 1232 (Mass. App. 1978)

A 77-year-old widow suffering from gangrene in her

right foot and lower leg refused to consent to a medically

recommended amputation of her leg even though such refusal

meant that she would probably die.  The physicians and hospital
sought court review after concluding that her decision was medically irrational.

The court found Mrs. Candura lucid at times and con-
fused at times, but she knew what the operation would entail and
the consequences of refusing it, thus there was no evidence that
her decision was uninformed or that she was "incapable of appre-
ciating the nature and consequences of her decision."  The court
made it clear that she was not required to agree with her physicians to be considered competent, even if every physician considered her decision medically irrational; as a competent person she had the right to refuse treatment, even life-saving
treatment.  The court also noted that neither her family nor her
physicians ever questioned her competence as long as she agreed
to their recommendations, as she had on two previous occasions
when she consented to less drastic amputations.

   c.  *Satz v. Perlmutter,* 362 So.2d 160 (Fla. Dist. Ct.
       App. 1978), aff'd, 379 S.2d 359 (Fla. 1980)

*Perlmutter* involved a 73-year-old man dying of amy-
otrophic lateral sclerosis (Lou Gehrig's disease).  He was expected to die within months, was bedridden, and depended on a
respirator.  He had tried to remove his respirator himself and
had expressed to his family his desire to avoid prolonging his
suffering.  The court rejected the State's claim that anyone

who disconnected the respirator would be guilty of assisting

suicide.  The court held:

> Abe Perlmutter should be allowed to make his choice to die
> with dignity, notwithstanding over a dozen legislative failures
> in this state to adopt suitable legislation in this field.  It
> is all very convenient to insist on continuing Mr. Perlmutter's
> life so that there can be no question of foul play, no result-
> ing civil liability and no possible trespass on medical ethics.
> However, it is quite another matter to do so at the patient's
> sole expense and against his competent will, thus inflicting
> never ending physical torture on his body until the inevitable,
> but artifically suspended, moment of death.  Such a course of
> conduct invades the patient's constitutional right of privacy,
> removes his freedom of choice and invades his right to self-
> determination.

3.   Incompetent Patients--Children

   a.   *Maine Medical Center v. Houle* (Sup. Ct., Cumberland
        Co., Maine, 74-145, Feb. 14, 1974)

Parents sought to refuse treatment for their new-

born who was born without a left eye, no ear canal, a malformed

thumb, and a tracheal-esophageal fistula.  Unless the fistula

was repaired, the infant could not be fed.  The court found

that "the most basic right enjoyed by every human being is the

right to life itself" and held that physicians had an obliga-

tion to preserve the life of an infant if treatment was "medi-

cally feasible."  Doctors could determine prognosis, but "the

doctor's qualitative evaluation of the value of the life to be

preserved is not legally within the scope of his expertise."

Once satisfied that the proposed treatment was "medically

necessary and medically feasible," the court ordered it to be
performed. (The child died a few days after the decision, before the operation could actually be performed.)

      b. *Custody of a Minor*, 379 N.E.2d 1053 (Mass. 1978)

      In this case, parental supplement of cancer chemo-
therapy with laetrile was ordered terminated on the basis that
the child, Chad Green, was being seriously harmed by the treatment and that it was unanimously opposed by the medical community. In a similar case in New York, *in re Hofbauer*, 56 A.D. 2d
108, 411, N.Y.S. 2d 416 (App. Div. 1978), metabolic therapy and
laetrile for Hodgkin's disease was approved where the child was
under the care of a licensed physician and the parents agreed
to revert to standard medical treatment if their child's health
deteriorated. (Both children were taken out of the country by
their parents and died shortly thereafter.)

      c. *In re Phillip Becker*, 156 Cal. Rptr. 48 (1st App.
         Dist., 1979)

      In July 1978, when this case first came to court,
Phillip Becker, a Down's syndrome child, was eleven years old.
The petition alleged that his parents were not providing him
with the "necessities of life," specifically a heart operation
to repair his ventricular septal defect. He had never lived
at home with his parents, but had been institutionalized since
birth. He was able to write his name, had good motor skills,

could converse reasonably and take part in school activities.
Two physicians testified in favor of the surgery, and one physician wrote a letter against it stating that in his opinion he
leads "a life I consider devoid of those qualities which give
it human dignity."  Phillip's parents opposed surgery on the
grounds that it would cause him to outlive them; because geri-
atric care is terrible, they feared that Phillip would not be
well cared for after they died.  They also did not want him to
be a burden on their other children.  The lower court judge was
conflicted, but because he found the treatment "elective" rather
than "a life-saving emergency," because it was risky, and because he did not know what he himself would do if he was the
parent of Phillip, he concluded that the parents' refusal was
"in the range of debatable actions."  The appeals court affirmed
this decision, stating there was "substantial evidence" to support the judge's conclusion.  Both the California Supreme Court
and the U.S. Supreme Court refused to review the case.

In a related action three years later, *Guardianship
of Phillip Becker* (Sup. Ct. Cal., Santa Clara Co., No. 101981,
Aug., 1981), a lower court granted partial guardianship of
Phillip to another couple and authorized them to reconsider the
issue of surgery.  That court said:  "The issue [in the former
proceedings] was too narrow, that is, the risk of surgery.  The
basic issue is and always has been one of parenting."

d. *State v. Perricone*, 37 N.J. 463, 181 A.2d 751 *cert. denied*,   371 U.S. 890 (1962)

*Perricone* involved the problem of parental refusal of treatment for an incompetent minor, in this case an infant requiring blood transfusions.  The parents refused to consent to the necessary transfusions on religious grounds, but the court held that religious freedom was not a sufficient justification for risking the death of a child:

> The right to practice religion freely does not include the liberty to expose . . . a child . . . to ill health or death. Parents may be free to become martyrs themselves.  But it does not follow they are free, in identical circumstances, to make martyrs of their children before they have reached the age of full and legal discretion when, they can make that choice for themselves.

4.   Incompetent Patients--Others

a. *Superintendent of Belchertown State School v. Saikewicz*, 370 N.E.2d 417 (Mass. 1977)

Joseph Saikewicz was a 67-year-old resident of a state school who was diagnosed as suffering from acute myeloblastic monocytic leukemia.  He had an IQ of 10, and his mental age was put at 2½.  With chemotherapy he had a 30-40% chance of a remission for 2-13 months; without treatment he would die within a matter of weeks or a few months at the most.  The lower court decided that because the chemotherapy had toxic side effects, including pain and discomfort, the low chance of success, his age and inability to cooperate, and the quality of his

life, the risks outweighed the benefits and he need not be
treated.  The Supreme Judicial Court of Massachusetts affirmed.
The Court followed the logic of the *Quinlan* opinion *(supra)* in
defining a constitutional right of privacy, the potential state
interests in restricting its exercise, and the right of an incompetent to refuse treatment based either on the objective
"best interests" test or the more subjective "substituted judgment" test, which it favored.  It rejected the "quality of life"
argument, except insofar as Mr. Saikewicz himself might take it
into account in making his own decision.  It decided Mr. Saikewicz need not be treated because, if he could make the decision
himself, the court believed he would opt for nontreatment,
therefore not treating him affirmed his autonomy.

On the issue of legal immunity, however, the court
departed from *Quinlan*, specifically rejecting the notion that an
"ethics committee" could confer legal immunity on physicians or
others:

We take a dim view of any attempt to shift the ultimate decision-making responsibility away from the duly established
courts of proper jurisdiction to any committee, panel or group,
ad hoc or permanent.  Thus, we reject the approached adopted by
the New Jersey Supreme Court in the *Quinlan* case of entrusting
the decision whether to continue artificial life support to the
patient's guardian, family, attending doctors, and hospital
"ethics committee."  70 N.J. at 55, 355 A.2d 647, 671.  One
rational for such a delegation was expressed by the lower court
judge in the *Quinlan* case, and quoted by the New Jersey Supreme
Court.  "The nature, extent and duration of care by societal
standards is the responsibility of a physician.  The morality
and conscience of our society places this responsibility in the
hands of the physician.  What justification is there to remove

it from the control of the medical profession and place it in
the hands of the courts?" *Id.* at 44, 355 A.2d at 665.  For its
part, the New Jersey Supreme Court concluded that "a practice
of applying to a court to confirm such decisions would generally
be inappropriate, not only because that would be a gratuitous
encroachment upon the medical profession's field of competence,
but because it would be impossibly cumbersome.  Such a requirement is distinguishable from the judicial overview traditionally
required in other matters such as the adjudication and commit-
ment of mental incompetents.  This is not to say that in the
case of an otherwise justifiable controversy access to the
courts would be foreclosed; we speak rather of a general practice and procedure." *Id.* at 50, 355 A.2d at 669.

  We do not view the judicial resolution of this most difficult and awesome question--whether potentially life-prolonging
treatment should be withheld from a person incapable of making
his own decision--as constituting a "gratuitous encroachment"
on the domain of medical expertise.  Rather, such questions of
life and death seem to us to require the process of detached
but passionate investigation and decision that forms the ideal
on which the judicial branch of government was created.  Achieving this ideal is our responsibility and that of the lower
court, and is not to be entrusted to any other group purporting
to represent the "morality and conscience of our society," no
matter how highly motivated or impressively constituted.

  b.  *In the Matter of Shirley Dinnerstein,* 380 N.E.2d
      134 (Mass. Appl. 1978)

        Mrs. Dinnerstein was diagnosed as suffering from

Alzheimer's disease in 1975, although she probably had been af-

flicted with it since 1972.  There is no cure, and death is in-

evitable, usually in five to seven years.  By November of 1975

she was completely disoriented; by February 1978 she had suf-

fered a massive stroke and was in essentially a vegetative

state, immobile and unaware of her environment.  Her life ex-

pectancy was less than a year and her attending physician be-

lieved that if she suffered a heart attack, she should not be resuscitated.  Her family, a physician son and a daughter with whom she had lived before being hospitalized, agreed.

The issue before the Appeals Court was whether a court order was necessary before an "order not to resuscitate" could be entered in her chart.  The court found that the *Saike-wicz* opinion neither "intended nor sanctioned" the requirement of prior judicial approval before the entry of a DNR order by a physician.  In the court's words:

> Such a situation presents a question peculiarly within the competence of the medical profession of what measures are appropriate to ease the imminent passing of an irreversibly, terminally ill patient in the light of the patient's history and condition and the wishes of her family.

### c. *Matter of Eichner and Matter of Storar*, 52 N.Y.2d 363 (1981)

These two very different cases were decided together by the New York Court of Appeals in March 1981.  The *Eichner* case (named for Brother Fox's religious superior) involved Brother Fox, an 83-year-old member of the Society of Mary who was being maintained on a respirator in a permanent vegetative state.  He had previously expressed orally a desire not to be maintained by "extraordinary means" (following the teachings of Pope Pius XII) if he were ever in a situation similar to Karen Ann Quinlan's.  Under these circumstances, the court concluded that Brother Fox had a common-law right to refuse treatment and that such refusal survives the incompetency of an individual if there is "clear and convincing evidence" of the refusal.

In Brother Fox's case the court concluded that his oral declarations were "solemn pronouncements" and not casual remarks. He was competent and therefore had the right to refuse treatment; his wishes must be respected: "Even in emergencies it is held that consent will not be implied if the patient has previously stated that he would not consent."

While Fox was a "*Quinlan*-type case," its companion, John *Storar*, was a "*Saikewicz* -type case," and therefore presented much more complex issues. John Storar was a profoundly retarded 52-year-old resident of a state facility and had the mental age of about 18 months. His closest relative was his mother, a 77-year-old widow. In July 1979 he was diagnoses as having bladde cancer and his mother was appointed his legal guardian to consent to radiation therapy, which produced a remission. Internal bleeding began in March 1980 and his bladder was unsuccessfully cauterized to stop it. At this point the cancer metastasized to his lungs, and he was considered terminal and inoperable. In May the physicians asked the mother for permission to administer blood transfusions. She reluctantly agreed, but in June, asked that the transfusions, which were given every two weeks, be discontinued. The director of the institution went to court to get an order to continue the blood transfusions. The mother opposed the petition. All the witnesses at the hearing agreed that Mr. Storar could not comprehend what was happening to him, that he had irreversible bladder cancer, and that even with the transfusions he could only live an estimated three to six months. Without them he would eventually bleed to death.

Mr. Storar found the transfusions disagreeable, and was distressed by the increased blood and clots in his urine after a transfusion. He had to be sedated and restrained at times before the transfusions, and received regular doses of painkillers.

Other experts testified that proper treatment involved administering only painkillers. Mrs. Storar testified that she only wanted her son to be comfortable, and since he obviously disliked the transfusions and tried to avoid them, she believed that he himself would want them discontinued. The lower court held that under these circumstances Mr. Storar's right to refuse treatment could be exercised by his mother because she was in the best position to determine what he would want. An intermediate appeals court affirmed.

But the New York Court of Appeals reversed the decision on the grounds that there was no realistic way to determine what John Storar himself would want done. Asking that question was, the court said, like asking, "If it snowed all summer, would it then be winter?" The court concluded that since John Storar was mentally an infant, he must be afforded

the same rights as an infant.  Since parents (even Jehovah's
Witnesses) cannot refuse life-saving blood transfusions for
their children, the court decided that Mrs. Storar could not refuse to have blood transfusions administered to her son.

## B.  Selected State Statutes on the Living Will

As of June 1982, eleven states and the District of Columbia
had adopted some form of "living will" or "right to die" legislation.  The provisions of these statutes vary (see diagram, pp.
76-77, but their primary purpose of them all is to provide immunity for physicians who honor prior directives of patients who
wish to refuse treatment if they become terminally ill and incompetent.  The first such statute to be passed was the California Natural Death Act.

### a.  California's Natural Death Act

Sec. 7186.  The Legislature finds that adult persons have the fundamental right to control the decisions relating to the rendering of their own medical care, including the
decision to have life-sustaining procedures withheld or withdrawn in instances of a terminal condition.
The Legislature further finds that modern medical
technology has made possible the artificial prolongation of
human life beyond natural limits.
The Legislature further finds that, in the interest
of protecting individual autonomy, such prolongation of life for
persons with a terminal condition may cause loss of patient dignity, and unnecessary pain and suffering, while providing nothing medically necessary or beneficial to the patient.
The Legislature further finds that there exists
considerable uncertainty in the medical and legal professions
as to the legality of terminating the use of application of

life-sustaining procedures where the patient has voluntarily and in sound mind evidenced a desire that such procedures be withheld or withdrawn.

In recognition of the dignity and privacy which patients have a right to expect, the Legislature hereby declares that the laws of the State of California shall recognize the right of an adult person to make a written directive instructing his physician to withhold or withdraw life-sustaining procedures in the event of a terminal condition.

Sec. 7187.  The following definitions shall govern the construction of this chapter:

(a)  "Attending physician" means the physician selected by, or assigned to, the patient who has primary responsibility for the treatment and care of the patient.

(b)  "Directive" means a written document voluntarily executed by the declarant in accordance with the requirements of Section 7188.  The directive, or a copy of the directive, shall be made part pf the patient's medical records.

(c)  "Life-sustaining procedure" means any medical procedure or intervention which utilizes mechancical or other artificial means to sustain, restore, or supplant a vital function, which, when applied to a qualified patient, would serve only to artifically prolong the moment of death and where, in the judgment of the attending physician, death is imminent whether or not such procedures are utilized.  "Life-sustaining procedure" shall not include the administration of medication or the performance of any medical procedure deemed necessary to alleviate pain.

(d)  "Physician" means a physician and surgeon licensed by the Board of Medical Quality Assurance or the Board of Osteopathic Examiners.

(e)  "Qualified patient" means a patient diagnosed and certified in writing to be afflicted with a terminal condition by two physicians, one of whom shall be the attending physician, who have personally examined the patient.

(f)  "Terminal condition" means an incurable condition caused by injury, disease, or illness, which, regardless of the application of life-sustaining procedures, would, within reasonable medical judgment, produce death, and where the

application of life-sustaining procedures
serves only to postpone the moment of death of
the patient.

Sec. 7188. Any adult person may execute a directive
directing the withholding or withdrawal of life-sustaining procedures in a terminal condition. The directive shall be signed
by the declarant in the presence of two witnesses not related
to the declarant by blood or marriage and who would not be entitled to any portion of the estate of the declarant upon his
decease under any will of the declarant or codicil thereto then
existing or, at the time of the directive, by operation of law
then existing. In addition, a witness to a directive shall not
be the attending physician, an employee of the attending physician or a health facility in which the declarant is a patient,
or any person who has a claim against any portion of the estate
of the declarant upon his decease at the time of the execution
of the directive. The directive shall be in the following form:

## DIRECTIVE TO PHYSICIANS

Directive made this _____ day of _____

I, _____, being of sound mind, willfully, and voluntarily make known my desire that my life shall not be artificially prolonged under the circumstances set forth below, do hereby declare:

1.  If at any time I should have an incurable injursy, di-
    sease, or illness certified to be a terminal condition
    by two physicians, and where the application of life-
    sustaining procedures would serve only to artifically
    prolong the moment of my death and where my physician
    determines that my death is imminent whether or not
    life-sustaining procedures are utilized, I direct that
    such procedures be withheld or withdrawn, and that I be
    permitted to die naturally.

2.  In the absence of my ability to give directions regard-
    ing the use of such life-sustaining procedures, it is my
    intention that this directive shall be honored by my
    family and physician(s) as the final expression of my
    legal right to refuse medical or surgical treatment and
    accept the consequences from such refusal.

3.  If I have been diagnosed as pregnant and that diagnosis
    is known to my physician, this directive shall have no
    force or effect during the course of my pregnancy.

4.  I have been diagnosed at least 14 days ago as having a terminal condition by _____, M.D., whose address is _____, and whose telephone number is _____. I understand that if I have not filled in the physician's name and address, it shall be presumed that I did not have a terminal condition when I made out this directive.

5.  This directive shall have no force or effect five years from the date filled in above.

6.  I understand the full import of this directive and I am emotionally and mentally competent to make this directive.

                              Signed _____
                    City, County and State of Residence

The declarant has been personally known to me and I believe him or her to be of sound mind.

            Witness_____          Witness_____

Sec. 7188.5  A directive shall have no force or effect if the declarant is a patient in a skilled nursing facility as defined in subdivision (c) of Section 1250 at the time the directive is executed unless one of the two witnesses to the directive is a patient advocate or ombudsman as may be designated by the State Department of Aging for this purpose pursuant to any other applicable provision of law. The patient advocate or ombudsman shall have the same qualifications as a witness under Section 7188.

The intent of this section is to recognize that some patients in skilled nursing facilities may be so insulated from a voluntary decision making role, by virtue of the custodial nature of their care, as to require special assurance that they are capable of willfully and voluntarily executing a directive.

Sec. 7189.  (a)  A directive may be revoked at any time by the declarant, without regard to his mental state or competency, by any of the following methods:

1.  By being canceled, defaced, obliterated, or burnt, torn, or otherwise destroyed by the declarant or by some person in his presence and by his direction.

2.  By a written revocation of the declarant expressing his intent to revoke, signed and dated by the declarant. Such revocation shall become

effective only upon communication to the attending physician by the declarant or by a person
acting on behalf of the declarant. The attending physician shall record in the patient's
medical record the time and date when he received notification of the written revocation.
3. By a veral expression by the declarant of his
intent to revoke the directive. Such revocation
shall become effective only upon communication
to the attending physician by the declarant or
by a person acting on behalf of the declarant.
The attending physician shall record in the patient's medical record the time, date, and place
of the revocation and the time, date, and place,
if different, of when he received notification
of the revocation.
(b) There shall be no criminal or civil liability
on the part of any person for failure to act
upon a revocation made pursuant to this section
unless that person has actual knowledge of the
revocation.

Sec. 7189.5  A directive shall be effective for five
years from the date of execution thereof unless sooner revoked
in a manner prescribed in Sec. 7189. Nothing in this chapter
shall be construed to prevent a declarant from reexecuting a
directive at any time in accordance with the formalities of Sec.
7188, including reexecution subsequent to a diagnosis of a terminal condition. If the declarant has executed more than one
directive, such time shall be determined from the date of execution of the last directive known to the attending physician.
If the declarant becomes comatose or is rendered incapable of
communicating with the attending physician, the directive shall
remain in effect for the duration of the comatose condition or
until such time as the declarant's condition renders him or her
able to communicate with the attending physician.

Sec. 7190.  No physician or health facility which,
acting in accordance with the requirements of this chapter,
causes the withholding or withdrawal of life-sustaining procedures from a qualified patient, shall be subject to civil
liability therefrom. No licensed health professional, acting
under the direction of a physician, who participates in the
withholding or withdrawal of life-sustaining procedures in accordance with the provisions of this chapter shall be subject
to any civil liability. No physician, or licensed health professional acting under the direction of a physician, who participates in the withholding or withdrawal of life-sustaining

procedures in according with the provisions of this chapter
shall be guilty of any crimincal act or of unprofessional conduct.

Sec. 7191. (a) Prior to effecting a withholding or
withdrawal of life-sustaining procedures from a qualified patient pursuant to the directive, the attending physician shall
determine that the directive complies with Sec. 7188, and, if
the patient is mentally competent, that the directive and all
steps proposed by the attending physician to be undertaken are
in accord with the desires of the qualified patient.

(b) If the declarant was a qualified patient at
least 14 days prior to executing or reexecuting
the directive, the directive shall be conclusively presumed, unlrdd revoked, to be the directions of the patient regarding the withholding or withdrawal of life-sustaining procedures.
No physician shall be criminally or civilly
liable for failing to effectuate the directive
of the qualified patient pursuant to this subdivision.  A failure by a physician to effectuate the directive of a qualified patient pursuant to this division shall constitute unprofessional conduct if the physician refuses to
make the necessary arrangements, or fails to
take the necessary steps, to effect the transfer
of the qualified patient to another physician
who will effectuate the directive of the qualified patient.

(c) If the declarant becomes a qualified patient subsequent to executing the directive, and has not
subsequently reexecuted the directive, the attending physician may give weight to the directive as evidence of the patient's directions regarding the withholding or withdrawal of life-
sustaining procedures and may consider other
factors, such as information from the affected
family or the nature of the patient's illness,
injury, or disease, in determining whether the
totality of circumstances known to the attending
physician justify effectuating the directive.
No physician, and no licensed health professional acting under the directive of a physician, shall be criminally or civilly liable for
failing to effectuate the directive of the
qualified patient pursuant to this subdivision.

Sec. 7192.  (a) The withholding or withdrawal of
life-sustaining procedures from a qualified patient in accordance with the provisions of this chapter shall not, for any
purpose, constitute a suicide.

(b) The making of a directive pursuant to Sec. 7188
shall not restrict, inhibit, or impair in any
manner the sale, procurement, or issuance of any
policy of life insurance, nor shall it be deemed
to modify the terms of an existing policy of
life insurance.  No policy of life insurance
shall be legally impaired or invalidated in any
manner by the withholding or withdrawal of life-
sustaining procedures from an insured qualified
patient, notwithstanding  any term of the policy
to the contrary.

(c) No physician, health facility, or other health
provider, and no health care service plan, in-
surer issuing disability insurance, self-in-
sured employee welfare benefit plan, or non-
profit hospital service plan, shall require any
person to execute a directive as a condition
for being insured for, or receiving, health care
services.

Sec. 7193.  Nothing in this chapter shall impair or
supersede any legal right or legal responsibility which any
person may have to effect the withholding or withdrawal of life-
sustaining procedures in any lawful manner.  In such respect
the provisions of this chapter are cumulative.

Sec. 7194.  Any person who willfully conceals, can-
cels, defaces, obliterates, or damages the directive of another
without such declarant's consent shall be guilty of a misdemeanor.  Any person, who, except where justified or excused by
law, falsifies or forges the directive of another, or willfully
concels or withholds personal knowledge of a revocation as provided in Section 7189, with the intent to cause a withholding
or withdrawal of life-sustaining procedures contrary to the
wishes of the declarant, and thereby, because of any such act,
directly causes life-sustaining procedures to be withheld or
withdrawn and death to thereby be hastened, shall be subject to
prosecution for unlawful homicide as provided in Chapter 1
(commencing with Section 187) of Title 8 of Part 1 of the Penal
Code.

Sec. 7195.  Nothing in this chapter shall be construed to condone, authorize, or approve mercy killing, or to
permit any affirmative or deliberate act or omission to end
life other than to permit the natural process of dying as provided in this chapter.

SECTION 2.  If any provision of this act or the application thereof to any person or circumstances is held invalid, such invalidity shall not affect other provisions or applications of the act which can be given effect without the invalid provision or application, and to this end the provisions of this act are severable.

SECTION 3.  Notwithstanding Section 2231 of the Revenue and Taxation Code, there shall be no reimbursement pursuant to this section nor shall there be any appropriation made by this act because of the Legislature recognizes that during any legislative session a variety of changes to laws relating to crimes and infractions may cause both increased and decreased costs to local government entities and school districts which, in the aggregate, do not result in significant identifiable cost changes.

b.  Washington's Natural Death Act

The 1981 Handbook of the Society for the Right to

Die (250 West 57th Street, New York, NY 10107) provides informa-

tion on the current status of state "natural death" legislation.

From it we reproduce this summary of the Washington Natural

Death Act and the two charts which follow.

The Washington Natural Death Act, sponsored by 20 state representatives and enacted in 1979, is a modification of the California Natural Death Act.  It has effectively eliminated most of the unnecessary restrictions contained in the California statute.
Washington's "Directive of Physicians" is legally binding whenever it is executed.  A directive must follow "essentially" the form contained in the law but may also include other specific directions.  Physicians and other health care professionals are protected from liability complying with the directive after confirmation of a terminal condition by two physicians.  If a physician refuses to effectuate the directive, he must make a "good faith effort" to transfer the qaulified patient to another physician but faces no penalty for failure to do so.
The Washington law retains an unfortunate requirement from its California model: medical procedures can be withheld or withdrawn only when "death is imminent."  This is a vague time factor and subject to a wide latitude of interpre-

tation.  It leaves considerable discretion as to the appropriate time for stopping some or all life-prolonging treatment because it is left to the judgment of the attending physician to determine when death is "imminent."

    c.  <u>Statutory Citations for Right-to-Die Laws</u>

Arkansas Act 879

      Ark. Stat. Ann. (1977 Supp.) Stat. 82-3801

      *et seq.*

California Natural Death Act (A.B. 3060)

      Cal. Stat. 1976, Chapt. 1439, Code §

      Health and Safety, § 7185  *et seq.*

Idaho Natural Death Act (S.B. 1164)

      Idaho Code 39-4501  *et seq.*

Kansas Senate Bill 99

      K.S.A. 65-128, 101-109 (1979 Supp.)

Nevada Assembly Bill 8

      Nev. Rev. Stat. § 449.540 *et seq.*

New Mexico Right to Die Act (S.B. 16)

      N.M. Stat. Ann. (1977 Supp.) § 12-35-1 *et seq.*

North Carolina Right to Natural Death (S.B. 504)

      N.C. Gen. Stat. 90-320 *et seq.*

Oregon Act "Rights with Respect to Terminal Illness" (S.B. 438)

      Or. Rev. Stat. § 97.050 *et seq.*

(continued on page 78)

| State | Became law | Time after which directive must be reexecuted | Form provided | Hospital and physician legally protected unless negligent | Binding on physician | Can be executed adult i good hea |
|---|---|---|---|---|---|---|
| Arkansas (Act 879) | July 1977 | None | No | Yes | Same as New Mexico | Yes |
| California (A.B. 3060) | Jan. 1977 | 5 years | Yes | Yes | Yes, if directive signed 14 days after patient becomes terminal | Yes, bu' binding unless patient termina |
| Idaho (S.B. 1164) | July 1977 | 5 years | Yes | Yes | Same as New Mexico (if patient is terminal and cannot communicate) | Same as Californ |
| Kansas (S 99) | April 1979 | None | Suggested form | Yes | Yes | Yes |
| Nevada (A.B. 8) | July 1977 | None | Yes | Yes | No | Yes |
| New Mexico (S.B. 16) | June 1977 | None | No | Yes, but physician must show "reasonable care and judgment" | Yes, but no penalty if physician does not comply | Yes |
| North Carolina (S.B. 504) | July 1977 | None | Yes | Physicians are protected; hospitals not specifically protected | No | Yes |
| Oregon (S.B. 438) | June 1977 | 5 years | Yes | Yes | Same as California | Same as Californ |
| Texas (S.B. 148) | Aug. 1977 | 5 years | Yes | Yes | Same as California | Same as Californ |
| Washington (H 264) | March 1979 | None | Suggested form | Yes | No | Yes |
| Alabama (Act 772) | May 1981 | None | Yes | Yes | Same as New Mexico | Yes |

| order to binding, st be re- uted after ient be- s terminal | Void while patient is pregnant | Provides for an agent to act on behalf of a minor | Provides for "ombudsman" for a patient in a skilled nursing facility | Provision for revocation | Penalties for hiding, destroying, or falsifying directive or revocation | Other provisions |
|---|---|---|---|---|---|---|
| No | No | Yes | No | No | No | Physician need not determine validity. Physician need not certify illness as terminal except for minors and incompetent patients. Proxy may act for incompetent patient. Signer may request life-sustaining procedures. |
| Yes | Yes | No | Yes | Yes | Yes | Physician must determine validity of directive and witnesses. Concealing evidence of revocation constitutes murder. Directive must be placed in patient's medical record. |
| Yes | No | No | No | Yes | No | Physician need not determine validity. Only operative if patient is comatose or unable to communicate with physician. Specifically does not cover persons not signing directives. |
| No | Yes | No | No | Yes | Yes | Physician need not determine validity. Patient has responsibility of notifying physician of existence of document. |
| but ctive is binding ny time) | Yes | No | No | Yes | Yes | Physician need not determine validity. Directive must be placed in patient's medical record. Similar documents executed before law went into effect "have same effect" as directives executed under the law. |
| No | No | Yes | No | Yes | Yes | Physician need not determine validity. Court must certify agent's decision when minor is involved. Minor may counter agent's decision. Directive must be placed in patient's medical record or physician's case file. |
| e as ada | No | No | No | Yes | No | Physician need not determine validity. Hospitals not specifically protected but can cite law as a defense. Clerk of court must validate directive. No age provisions. Brain death defined. |
| es | No | No | Yes | Yes | Yes | Physician need not determine validity. Directive must be placed in patient's medical record. |
| es | Yes | No | No | Yes | Yes | Basically the same as the California law except (1) physician need not determine validity and (2) no provision for ombudsman for patients in skilled nursing facilities. |
| o | Yes | No | No | Yes | Yes | Physician need not determine validity. Patient has responsibility of notifying physician of existence of document. |
| o | Yes | No | No | Yes | Yes | Physician must be responsible for providing written certification and declarant confirmation of the terminal condition. |

Texas Natural Death Act (S.B. 148)

Vernon's Ann. Civ. St. Art. 4590h § 1 *et seq.*

Washington Natural Death Act (H.B. 264)

Rev. Code of Wash. 70.122.01 *et seq.* (1980

Supp.)

## C. Policy Statements

### a. Address of Pope Pius XII (1957)

In this address, Pope Pius XII distinguished between "ordinary" and "extraordinary" means of life-prolonging
treatment. He stated that:

When inevitable death is imminent in spite of the
means used, it is permitted in conscience to take the decision
to refuse forms of treatment that would only secure a pre-
carious and burdensome prolongation of life.

### b. Neasden Hospital Order (1965)

A sign posted on a bulletin board in Neasden Hospital in Great Brtain was an early example of specific orders
not to resuscitate:

The following patients are not to be resuscitated:
those who are very elderly (over 65 years of age); those who
are suffering from malignant disease; those with chronic chest
disease; and those with chronic renal disease.

### c. Ethical and Religious Directives for Catholic Health Facilities (1971)

A report of the National Conference of Catholic

Bishops and the United States Catholic Conference, Department

of Health Affairs, United States Catholic Conference (November,

1971) states that the "directly intended termination of any pa-

tient's life, even at his own request, is always morally wrong."

     d.   A Patient's Bill of Rights (1973)

          Item Four of the American Medical Association's

"Patient's Bill of Rights" discusses the right to refuse treat-

ment:  "The patient has the right to refuse treatment to the

extent permitted by law, and to be informed of the medical con-

sequences of his action." [American Hospital Association, Hos-

pitals, Vol. 4, No. 4 (Feb. 16, 1973)]

     e.   The Rights and Responsibilities of Christians Re-
          garding Human Death (1973)

          From the statement of Christian concern addressed

to the Churches of the Ninth General Synod of the United Church

of Christ, adopted June 25, 1973:

>      Nothing in Jewish or Christian traditions or in
> medical ethics presumes that a physician has a mandate to impose
> his or her wishes and skills upon patients for the sake of pro-
> longing the length of their dying where those patients are di-
> agnosed as terminally ill and do not wish the interventions of
> the physician.  People who are dying have as much freedom as
> other living persons to accept or to refuse medical treatment
> where that treatment provides no cure for their ailment.  Thus
> the freedom of the patient to choose his own style for the re-
> mainder of his life and the method and time for dying is en-
> hanced.  Here the illness, or, depending on one's theology, God,
> has already made death imminent.
>      Some people realize that when the time comes for a
> specific decision in their terminal illness they may be coma-
> tose and unable to make their wish known.  To prepare for this
> contingency while still in good mental health, they may sign a

"living will," or a document like a will in its formalities, or
a formal direction to a guardian or committee appointed to represent them while non compos mentis, expressing their desire or
stating their orders that they may not be kept alive by artificial means or "heroic measures" and requesting that drugs be
administered to alleviate terminal suffering even if they hasten
the moment of death.  While not legally binding under present
law, such a document is a responsible act to the family, the
attending physician, and clergy.
        We believe it is ethically and theologically proper
for a person to wish to avoid artificial and/or painful prolongation of a terminal illness and for him or her to execute
a living will or similar document of instructions.  It must be
recognized, however, that such a document, at times, may work
to the harm of the patient.


        f.   1974 United States Catholic Conference Document

        In this report, "extraordinary means" of prolonging

life were defined to be "all medicines, treatments and opera-

tions which cannot be obtained or used without excessive pain,

expense or inconveniences or which, if used, would not offer

reasonable hope of benefit."


        g.   1974 Standards of Cardio-Pulmonary Resuscitation
             and Emergency Cardiac Care

        From the National Conference on Cardiopulmonary

Resuscitation (a collaboration of the American Heart Associa-

tion and the National Science Foundation):

        Cardiopulmonary resuscitation is not indicated in
certain situations, such as in cases of terminal irreversible
illness where death is not unexpected or where prolonged cardiac arrest dictates the futility of resuscitation efforts . . . .
When CPR is considered to be contraindicated for hospital patients, it is appropriate to indicate this in the patient's
progress notes.  It also is appropriate to indicate this on the
physician's order sheet for the benefit of nurses and other
personnel who may be called upon to  initiate or participate
in cardiopulmonary resuscitation.

h.  <u>New York Presbytery Statement</u> (1976)

From a pastoral letter written "to reflect upon the

issue of euthanasia in the light of Christian faith and pastoral

concern" (March 9, 1976):

> We support euthanasia (defined as the refusal to
> take extraordinary means to preserve life) when one has been re-
> duced to a vegetative existence or is dying of an incurable di-
> sease with unrelieved suffering.
>
> Most of all, we affirm that no individual ought to
> be left alone to make those decisions where the question of
> innocence or guilt might become the burden of one person.  The
> medical and legal professions alone should not bear the burden,
> nor usurp the authority, of deciding for others "the right to
> die."  The person who is dying, the family, friends, or others
> who are involved--after consultation with competent medical and
> legal authorities--should have the right to decide when extra-
> ordinary life-sustaining measures shall be withdrawn.

i.  <u>Declaration on Euthanasia</u> (1980)

Adopted by the Sacred Congregation for the Doctrine

of the Faith, approved by Pope John Paul II, May 5, 1980, this

eight-page statement outlined the Vatican's policy toward eu-

thanasia.  Two excerpts follow:

> Today it is very important to protect, at the mo-
> ment of death, both the dignity of the human person and the
> Christian concept of life, against a technical attitude that
> threatens to become an abuse,  Thus, some people speak of a
> "right to die", which is an expression that does not mean the
> right to procure death either by one's own hand or by means of
> someone else, as one pleases, but rather the right to die peace-
> fully with human and Christian dignity.  From this point of
> view, the use of therapeutic means can sometimes pose problems.
>
> It is also permissible to make due with the normal
> means that medicine can offer.  Therefore one cannot impose on
> anyone the obligation to have recourse to a technique which is
> already in use but which carries a risk or is burdensome.  Such

a refusal is not the equivalent of suicide; on the contrary, it
should be considered as an acceptance of the human condition,
or a wish to avoid the application of a medical procedure dis-
proportionate to the results that can be expected, or a desire
not to impose excessive expense on the family or the community.

      j.   Current Opinions of the Judicial Council of the
          American Medical Association (1981)

      Where a terminally ill patient's coma is beyond
doubt irreversible and there are adequate safeguards to confirm
the accuracy of the diagnosis, all means of life support may be
discontinued.

      k.   The American Public Health Association on Death
          with Dignity (1981)

      Resolution of the American Public Health Associa-

tion, adopted by its Governing Council at the APHA annual meet-

ing, November, 1981:

      Recognizing that to the seriously ill and infirm,
death is not only a distinct possibility, but sometimes preferable to any alternative; and
      Believing that health care policy should emphasize
the quality of life and dignity of death and assure self-determination and the right to refuse treatment and not blindly
stress the continuation of life; and
      Noting that a technologically-oriented health sys-
tem frequently supports the futile prolongation of dying and
ignores the emotional as well as physical needs of the terminally ill and their families; and
      Believing that a national policy on long-term care
would be grossly inadequate without recognizing the patient's
right to die; therefore
      Encourages states and the federal government to
pass model "Right to Refuse Medical Treatment" legislation
(similar bills have been passed in 12 states) which
               * spells out a general right of the patient to
                 refuse treatment of all kinds without the need
                 for certification of a terminal condition;
               * provides that this right be exercised in a
                 document that takes legal effect after patient
                 incompetency;

      * provides for the naming of a person to help
        exercise this right after patient incompetency;
        and
      * provides for legal immunity for following the
        patient's wishes, as well as civil and criminal
        penalties for ignoring them; and
    Encourages the concepts of the "living will" and
"ethics committees" in hospitals and other health facilities as
examples of ways this policy may be implemented; and
    Supports further study to better delineate the
ethical, legal, and medical issues involved in the concept of
the right to die.

# III.  DETERMINATION OF DEATH

## A.  Policy Statements

### 1.  "A Definition of Irreversible Coma"

This "Report of the Ad Hoc Committee of the Harvard Medical
School to Examine the Definition of Brain Death" was published
in the *Journal of the American Medical Association* 205:337-340
(1968).

> Our primary purpose is to define irreversible coma as a new
> criterion for death.  There are two reasons why there is need
> for a definition: (1) Improvements in resuscitative and support-
> ive measures have led to increased efforts to save those who are
> desperately injured.  Sometimes these efforts have only partial
> success so that the result is an individual whose heart contin-
> ues to beat but whose brain is irreversibly damaged.  The burden
> is great on patients who suffer permanent loss of intellect, on
> their families, on the hospitals, and on those in need of hospi-
> tal beds already occupied by these comatose patients.  (2) Obso-
> lete criteria for the definition of death can lead to controver-
> sy in obtaining organs for transplantation.
>
> Irreversible coma has many causes, but *we are concerned here
> only with those comatose individuals who have no discernible cen-
> tral nervous system activity*.  If the characteristics can be de-
> fined in satisfactory terms, translatable into action--and we be-
> lieve this is possible--then several problems will either disap-
> pear or will become more readily soluble.
>
> More than medical problems are present.  There are moral,
> ethical, religious, and legal issues.  Adequate definition here
> will prepare the way for better insight into all of these mat-
> ters as well as for better law than is currently applicable.

> Characteristics of Irreversible Coma

> An organ, brain or other, that no longer functions and has

no possibility of functioning again is for all practical purposes
dead.  Our first problem is to determine the characteristics of a
*permanently* nonfunctioning brain.

A patient in this state appears to be in deep coma.  The condition can be satisfactorily diagnosed by points 1, 2, and 3 to
follow.  The electroencephalogram (point 4) provides confirmatory
data, and when available it should be utilized.  In situations
where for one reason or another electroencephalographic monitoring is not available, the absence of cerebral function has to be
determined by purely clinical signs, to be described, or by absence of circulation as judged by standstill of blood in the ret-
inal vessels, or by absence of cardiac activity.

1. *Unreceptivity and Unresponsivity.*--There is a total una-
wareness to externally applied stimuli and inner need and complete unresponsiveness--our definition of irreversible coma.
Even the most intensely painful stimuli evoke no vocal or other
response, not even a groan, withdrawal of a limb, or quickening
of respiration.

2. *No Movements or Breathing.*--Observations covering a period
of at least one hour by physicians is adequate to satisfy the criteria of no spontaneous muscular movements or spontaneous respiration or response to stimuli such as pain, touch, sound, or
light.  After the patient is on a mechanical respirator, the total absence of spontaneous breathing may be established by turning off the respirator for three minutes and observing whether
there is any effort on the part of the subject to breathe spon-
taneously.  (The respirator may be turned off for this time provided that at the start of the trial period the patien's carbon
dioxide tension is within the normal range, and provided also
that the patient had been breathing room air for at least 10 minutes prior to the trial.)

3. *No reflexes.*--Irreversible coma with abolition of central
nervous system activity is evidenced in part by the absence of
elicitable reflexes.  The pupil will be fixed and dilated and
will not respond to a direct source of bright light.  Since the
establishment of a fixed, dilated pupil is clear-cut in clinical
practice, there should be no uncertainty as to its presence.
Ocular movement (to head turning and to irrigation of the ears
with ice water) and blinking are absent.  There is no evidence of
postural activity (decerebrate or other).  Swallowing, yawning,
vocalization are in abeyance.  Corneal and pharyngeal reflexes
are absent.

As a rule the stretch of tendon reflexes cannot be elicited;
ie, tapping the tendons of the biceps, triceps, and pronator muscles, quadriceps and gastrocnemius muscles with the reflex ham-
mer elicits no contraction of the respective muscles.  Plantar or
noxious stimulation gives no response.

4. *Flat Electroencephalogram.*--Of great confirmatory value is
the flat or isoelectric EEG.  We must assume that the electrodes

have been properly applied, that the apparatus is functioning normally, and that the personnel in charge is competent.  We consider it prudent to have one channel of the apparatus used for an
electrocardiogram.  This channel will monitor the ECG so that, if
it appears in the electroencephalographic leads because of high
resistance, it can be readily identified.  It also establishes
the presence of the active heart in the absence of the EEG.  We
recommend that another channel be used for a noncephalic lead.
This will pick up space-borne or vibration-borne artifacts and
identify them.  The simplest form of such a monitoring noncephalic electrode has two leads over the dorsum of the hand, preferably the right hand, so the ECG will be minimal or absent.  Since
one of the requirements of this state is that there be no muscle
activity, these two dorsal hand electrodes will not be bothered
by muscle artifact.  The apparatus should be run at standard
gains $10\mu v/mm$, $50\mu v/5\ mm$.  Also it should be isoelectric at dou-
ble this standard gain which is $5\mu v/mm$ or $25\mu v/5mm$.  At least ten
full minutes of recording are desirable, but twice that would be
better.

It is also suggested that the gains at some point be opened
to their full amplitude for a brief period (5 to 100 seconds) to
see that is going on.  Usually in an intensive care unit artifacts will dominate the picture, but these are readily identifiable.  There shall be no electroencephalographic response to
noise or to pinch.

All of the above tests shall be repeated at least 24 hours
later with no change.

The validity of such data as indications of irreversible cerebral damage depends on the exclusion of two conditions: hypo-
thermia (temperature below 90°F [32.2°C]) or central nervous system depressants, such as barbiturates.

## Other Procedures

The patient's condition can be determined only by a physician.  When the patient is hopelessly damaged as defined above,
the family and all colleagues who have participated in major decisions concerning the patient, and all nurses involved, should
be so informed.  Death is to be declared and *then* the respirator
turned off.  The decision to do this and the responsibility for
it are to be taken by the physician-in-charge, in consultation
with one or more physicians who have been directly involved in
the case.  It is unsound and undesirable to force the family to
make the decision.

## Legal Commentary

The legal system of the United States is greatly in need of
the kind of analysis and recommendations for medical procedures

in cases of irreversible brain damage as described.  At present,
the law of the United States, in all 50 states and in the federal
courts, treats the question of human death as a question of fact
to be decided in every case.  When any doubt exists, the courts
seek medical expert testimony concerning the time of death of the
particular individual involved.  However, the law makes the assumption that the medical criteria for determining death are settled and not in doubt among physicians.  Furthermore, the law as-
sumes that the traditional method among physicians for determination of death is to ascertain the absence of all vital signs.
To this extent, *Black's Law Dictionary* (fourth edition, 1951) de-
fines death as

> The cessation of life; the ceasing to exist; *defined by phy-
> sicians* as a total stoppage of the circulation of the blood,
> and a cessation of the animal and vital functions consequent
> thereupon, such as respiration, pulsation, etc [italics
> added].

In the few modern court decisions involving a definition of
death, the courts have used the concept of the total cessation of
all vital signs.  Two cases are worthy of examination.  Both involved the issue of which one of two persons died first.

In *Thomas vs Anderson*, (96 Cal App 2d 371, 211 P 2d 478) a
California District Court of Appeal in 1950 said, "In the instant
case the question as to which of the two men died first was a
question of fact for the determination of the trial court..."

The appellate court cited and quoted in full the definition
of death from *Black's Law Dictionary* and concluded, "...death occurs precisely when life ceases and does not occur until the
heart stops beating and respiration ends.  Death is not a con-
tinuous event and is an event that takes place at a precise
time."

The other case is *Smith vs Smith* (229 Ark, 579, 317 SW 2d
275) decided in 1958 by the Supreme Court of Arkansas.  In this
case the two people were husband and wife involved in an auto accident.  The husband was found dead at the scene of the accident.
The wife was taken to the hospital unconscious.  It is alleged
that she "remained in coma due to brain injury" and died at the
hospital 17 days later.  The petitioner in court tried to argue
that the two people died simultaneously.  The judge writing the
opinion said the petition contained a "quite unusual and unique
allegation."  It was quoted as follows:

> That the said Hugh Smith and his wife, Lucy Coleman Smith,
> were in an automobile accident on the 19th day of April,
> 1957, said accident being instantly fatal to each of them
> at the same time, although the doctors maintained a vain
> hope of survival and made every effort to revive and resus-

citate said Lucy Coleman Smith until May 6th, 1957, when it
was finally determined by the attending physicians that their
hope of resuscitation and possible restoration of human life
to the said Lucy Coleman Smith was entirely vain, and
    That as a matter of modern medical science, your peti-
tioner alleges and states, and will offer the Court competent
proof that the said Hugh Smith, deceased, and said Lucy Coleman Smith, deceased, lost their power to will at the same instant, and that their demise as earthly human beings occurred
at the same time in said automobile accident, neither of them
ever regaining any consciousness whatsoever.

The court dismissed the petition as a *matter of law*.  The
court quoted *Black's* definition of death and concluded,

    Admittedly, this condition did not exist, and as a matter of
    fact, it would be too much of a strain of credulity for us to
    believe any evidence offered to the effect that Mrs. Smith
    was dead, scientifically or otherwise, unless the conditions
    set out in the definition existed.

Later in the opinion the court said, "Likewise, we take judicial notice that one breathing, though unconscious, is not dead."
    "Judicial notice" of this definition of death means that the
court did not consider that definition open to serious controversy; it considered the question as settled in responsible scientific and medical circles.  The judge thus makes proof of uncon-
troverted facts unnecessary so as to prevent prolonging the
trial with unnecessary proof and also to prevent fraud being committed upon the court by quasi "scientists" being called into
court to controvert settled scientific principles at a price.
Here, the Arkansas Supreme Court considered the definition of
death to be a settled, scientific, biological fact.  It refused
to consider the plaintiff's offer of evidence that "modern medical science" might say otherwise.  In simplified form, the above
is the state of the law in the United States concerning the definition of death.
    In this report, however, we suggest that responsible medical
opinion is ready to adopt new criteria for pronouncing death to
have occurred in an individual sustaining irreversible coma as
a result of permanent brain damage.  If this position is adopted
by the medical community, it can form the basis for change in the
current legal concept of death.  No statutory change in the law
should be necessary since the law treats this question essentially as one of fact to be determined by physicians.  The only circumstance in which it would be necessary that legislation be offered in the various states to define "death" by law would be in
the event that great controversy were engendered surrounding the
subject and physicians were unable to agree on the new medical

criteria.

It is recommended as a part of these procedures that judgment of the existence of these criteria is solely a medical issue. It is suggested that the physician in charge of the patient consult with one or more other physicians directly involved in the case before the patient is declared dead on the basis of these criteria. In this way, the responsibility is shared over a wider range of medical opinion, thus providing an important degree of protection against later questions which might be raised about the particular case. It is further suggested that the decision to declare the person dead, and then to turn off the respirator, be made by physicians not involved in any later effort to transplant organs or tissue from the deceased individual. This is advisable in order to avoid any appearance of self-interest by the physicians involved.

It should be emphasized that we recommend the patient be declared dead before any effort is made to take him off a respirator, if he is then on a respirator. This declaration should not be delayed until he has been taken off the respirator and all artificially stimulated signs have ceased. The reason for this recommendation is that in our judgment it will provide a greater degree of legal protection to those involved. Otherwise, the physicians would be turning off the respirator on a person who is, under the present strict, technical application of the law, still alive.

### 2.  Declaration of Sydney

Adopted by the 22nd World Medical Assembly, Sydney, Australia, August 1968, was the following "Statement on Death":

1. The determination of the time of death is in most countries the legal responsibility of the physician and should remain so. Usually he will be able without special assistance to decide that a person is dead, employing the classical criteria known to all physicians.

2. Two modern practices in medicine, however, have made it necessary to study the question of the time of death further; (a) the ability to maintain by artificial means the circulation of oxygenated blood through tissues of the body which may have been irreversibly injured and (b) the use of cadaver organs such as heart or kidneys for transplantation.

3. A complication is that death is a gradual process at the cellular level with tissues varying in their ability to withstand deprivation of oxygen. But clinical interest lies not in the state of preservation of isolated cells but in the fate of a per-

son.  Here the point of death *of the different cells and organs*
is not so important as the certainty that the process has become
irreversible by whatever techniques of resuscitation may be employed.

4. This determination will be based on clinical judgment supplemented *if necessary* by a number of diagnostic aids of which
the electroencephalograph is currently the most helpful.  However, no single technological criterion is entirely satisfactory
in the present state of medicine nor can any one technological
procedure be substituted for the overall judgment of the physician.  *If transplantation of an organ is involved, the decision
that death exists should be made by two or more physicians and
the physicians determining the moment of death should in no way
be immediately concerned with performance of transplantation.*

5. Determination of the point of death of the person makes it
ethically permissible to cease attempts at resuscitation and in
countries where the law permits, to remove organs from the cadaver provided that prevailing legal requirements of consent have
been fulfilled.


3.  Defining Death:  Medical, Legal and Ethical Issues in
    the Determination of Death

The July 1981 Report of the President's Commission for the

Study of Ethical Problems in Medicine and Biomedical and Behav-

ioral Research (Suite 555, 2000 K Street N.W., Washington, DC

20006) concluded as follows:

The enabling legislation for the President's Commission directs it to study "the ethical and legal implications of the matter of defining death, including the advisability of developing
a uniform definition of death."  In performing its mandate, the
Commission has reached conclusions on a series of questions
which are the subject of this Report.  In summary, the central
conclusions are:

1. That recent developments in medical treatment necessitate
a restatement of the standards traditionally recognized for determining that death has occurred.

2. That such a restatement ought preferably to be a matter
of statutory law.

3. That such a statute ought to remain a matter for state
law, with federal action at this time being limited to areas under current federal jurisdiction.

4. That the statutory law ought to be uniform among the sev-

eral states.

5. That the "definition" contained in the statute ought to address general physiological standards rather than medical criteria and tests, which will change with advances in biomedical knowledge and refinements in technique.

6. That death is a unitary phenomenon which can be accurately demonstrated either on the traditional grounds of irreversible cessation of heart and lung functions or on the basis of irreversible loss of all functions of the entire brain.

7. That any statutory "definition" should be kept separate and distinct from provisions governing the donation of cadaver organs and from any legal rules on decisions to terminate life-sustaining treatment.

To embody these conclusions in statutory form the Commission worked with the three organizations which had proposed model legislation on the subject, the American Bar Association, the American Medical Association, and the National Conference of Commissioners on Uniform State Laws. These groups have now endorsed the following statute, in place of their previous proposals:

Uniform Determination of Death Act

An individual who has sustained either (1) irreversible cessation of circulatory and respiratory functions, or (2) irreversible cessation of all functions of the entire brain, including the brain stem, is dead. A determination of death must be made in accordance with accepted medical standards.

The Commission recommends the adoption of this statute in all jurisdictions in the United States.

B.  Judicial Decisions

It is not much of an exaggeration to say that courts have

traditionally accepted whatever definition of death was accept-

able to the medical community. Put another way, the law is: A

person is dead when the doctor says they are dead (so long as

the doctor makes this determination based on accepted medical

standards). The following cases illustrate this judicial accep-

tance of medical practice in both the criminal and civil context.

1. *State v. Fierro*, 124 Ariz. 182, 603 P.2d 74 (1979)

The defendant sought to avoid a murder conviction by arguing that it was not the gunshot wound he inflicted, but the physician's removal of life-support equipment that ended the life of the victim. The court disagreed, holding that although the common-law standard (cessation of spontaneous heartbeat and respiration) was still sufficient to determine death, the medical criteria advanced by the ad hoc Harvard Committee, or the legal standard put forward in the Uniform Brain Death Act (*infra*) were also valid bases for determining death so long as they were properly supported by medical testimony.

2. *People v. Saldana*, 47 Cal. App. 3d 954, 121 Cal. Rptr. 243 (1975)

In this murder case, a physician testified that death is "a failure of part of that organism such that the total organism is no longer functioning in a manner which a reasonable, intelligent person would recognize as the purpose of that organism." In the absence of any testimony to contradict the physician's testimony that the victim had suffered brain death, the court held that the victim's death was caused by the defendant's criminal act: "Given the current state of medical science . . . we cannot say as a matter of law that the victim was not dead when he reached the hospital, much less when the artificial life-support systems were removed."

3.  *Commonwealth v. Golston*, 373 Mass. 249, 366 N.E.2d 744
    (1977), *cert. denied*, 434 U.S. 1039 (1978)

The trial judge in this murder case instructed the jury that,
"as a matter of law, the occurrence of a brain death, if you find
it, satisfies the essential element of the crime of murder requiring proof beyond a reasonable doubt of the death of the victim." Massachusetts had no brain death statute, so the judge
continued his instruction using the language of statutes from
other jurisdictions: "Brain death occurs when, in the opinion of
a licensed physician, based on ordinary and accepted standards of
medical practice, there has been a total and irreversible cessation of spontaneous brain functions and further attempts at resuscitation or continued supportive maintenance would not be suc-
cessful in restoring such functions."

The Supreme Judicial Court of Massachusetts concluded that
the trial judge had acted correctly in accepting the medical concept of brain death as the legal standard.


4.  *Lovato v. District Ct.*, 601 P.2d 1072 (Colo. 1979) (en
    banc)

*Lovato* adopted the brain death criteria as an alternative
standard for determining death. The trial judge held that:

(A)s the rule of this case . . . to be followed until otherwise
changed legally or judicially, we adopt the provisions of the
proposed Uniform (Brain Death) Act. . . . Our recognition of
this concept of brain death does not preclude continuing recognition of the standard of death as determined by traditional criteria of cessation of respiration and circulation.

The Colorado Supreme Court upheld the District Court ruling and

added:

We recognize the authority of, and indeed encourage, the General
Assembly to pronounce statutorily the standards by which death is
to be determined in Colorado.  We do not, however, believe that
in the absence of legislative action we are precluded from facing
and resolving the legal issue of whether irretrievable loss of
brain function can be used as a means of detecting the condition
of death.  Under the circumstances of this case we are not only
entitled to resolve the question, but have a duty to do so.  To
act otherwise would be to close our eyes to the scientific and
medical advances made worldwide in the past two or three decades.


   5.  *In re Bowman*, 617 P.2d 731 (Wash. 1980)

Five-year-old Matthew Bowman had suffered massive physical

injuries from a non-family-member who was caring for him.  He

was admitted to the hospital in critical condition and placed

under the guardianship of the Department of Social and Health

Services.  When his natural parents were located, his court-ap-

pointed guardian objected to being dismissed because the parents

were going to order that medical support for Matthew be stopped.

Even though the trial court ruled that Matthew was dead, it en-

joined the removal of "extraordinary measures" pending appeal.

The day before appellate argument, Matthew's heart ceased beating

and his heartbeat could not be restored.  The court nevertheless

reviewed the case, and determined, on the basis of medical testi-

mony that "Matthew's brain was dead under the most rigid criteria

available, the 'Harvard criteria' . . . [and] all physicians in

the Children's Orthopedic Hospital intensive care unit agreed

. . . that Matthew was no longer alive" at the time of the hearing.

Based on this testimony, the Washington Supreme Court "adopted" the Uniform Determination of Death Act standards (*infra*) as
the state's legal standard for death, while leaving to the medical profession the definition of "acceptable diagnostic tests and
medical procedures . . . taking into account new knowledge of
brain function and new diagnostic procedures."


## C.  State Statutes


### 1.  Selected Statutes

Approximately 30 states have adopted some definition of brain
death by statute.  More than 20 are based on the models set forth
in section 2 *infra*, and it is likely that most, if not all, future statutes on this subject will be based on the Uniform  Determination of Death Act model.


#### a.  Kansas Stat. Ann. 77-202 (Supp. 1971)

A person will be considered medically and legally dead, if
in the opinion of a physician, based on ordinary standards of medical practice, there is the absence of spontaneous respiratory
and cardiac function and, because of the disease or condition
which caused, directly or indirectly, these functions to cease,
or because of the passage of time since these functions ceased,
attempts at resuscitation are considered hopeless; and, in this
event, death will have occurred at the time these functions
ceased; or
A person will be considered medically and legally dead if, in
the opinion of a physician, based on ordinary standards of medi-

cal practice, there is the absence of spontaneous brain function;
and if based on ordinary standards of medical practice, during
reasonable attempts to either maintain or restore spontaneous circulatory or respiratory function in the absence of aforesaid
brain function, it appears that further attempts at resuscitation
or supportive maintenance will not succeed, death will have occurred at the time when these conditions first coincide.  Death is
to be pronounced before artificial means of supporting respiratory and circulatory function are terminated and before any vital
organ is removed for purpose of transplantation.
  These alternative definitions of death are to be utilized for
all purposes in this state, including the trials of civil and criminal cases, any laws to the contrary notwithstanding.

  States that have adopted modified versions of the Kansas stat-

ute are Maryland (1972), New Mexico (1973), and Virginia (1973).

###  b.   Alaska Stat. $ 09.65.120 (Cum. Supp. 1980)

  A person is considered medically and legally dead if, in the
opinion of a medical doctor licensed or exempt from licensing under AS 08.64, based on ordinary standards of medical practice,
there is no spontaneous respiratory or cardiac function and
there is no expectation of recovery of spontaneous respiratory
or cardiac function or, in the case when respiratory and cardiac
functions are maintained by articial means, a person is considered medically and legally dead, if, in the opinion of a medical
doctor licensed or exempt from licensing under AS 08.64, based on
ordinary standards of medical practice, there is no spontaneous
brain function.  Death may be pronounced in this circumstance
before artificial means of maintaining respiratory and cardiac
function are terminated.

###  c.   Arkansas Stat. Ann. §§82-537--82-538 (Cum. Supp. 1981; effective February 11, 1979)

  A person is legally dead when the brain has irreversibly
ceased to function and there is an absence of spontaneous breath.

  The diagnosis of death as defined in this ACT [§§ 82-537, 82-
538] shall be made using ordinary standards of medical practice.

d. California Health & Safety Code §§ 7180-7182 (Deering Supp. 1980)

A person shall be pronounced dead if it is determined by a physician that the person has suffered a total and irreversible cessation of brain function. There shall be independent confirmation of the death by another physician.

Nothing in this chapter shall prohibit a physician from using other usual and customary procedures for determining death as the exclusive basis for pronouncing a person dead.

When a part of the donor is used for direct transplantation pursuant to the Uniform Anatomical Gift Act (Chapter 3.5, commencing with Section 7150) and the death of the donor is determined by determining that the person has suffered a total and irreversible cessation of brain function there shall be an independent confirmation of the death by another physician. Neither the physician making the determination of death under Section 7155.5 nor the physician making the independent confirmation shall participate in the procedures for removing or transplanting a part.

Complete patient medical records required of a health facility pursuant to regulations adopted by the department in accordance with Section 1275 shall be kept, maintained, and preserved with respect to the requirements of this chapter when a person is pronounced dead by determining that the person has suffered a total and irreversible cessation of brain function.

e. Montana Rev. Codes Ann. § 50-22-101 (1978)

A human body with irreversible cessation of total brain function as determined according to usual and customary standards of medical practice, is dead for all legal purposes.

2. Model Statutes

The model statutes and comments that follow are quoted from

the July 1981 Report of the President's Commission for the Study

of Ethical Problems in Medicine and Biomedical and Behavioral Re-

search entitled *Defining Death: Medical, Legal and Ethical Is-*

*sues in the Determination of Death.*

### a.  Uniform Brain Death Act

The following is a proposal approved and recommended for enactment by the National Conference of Commissioners on Uniform
State Laws at its Annual Conference on July 28-August 4, 1978:

*Section 1.* [*Brain Death.*]  For legal and medical purposes, an
individual who has sustained irreversible cessation of all functioning of the brain, including the brain stem, is dead.  A determination under this section must be made in accordance with reasonable medical standards.

### Comment

This section legislates the concept of brain death.  The Act
does not preclude a determination of death under other legal or
medical criteria, including the traditional criteria of cessation
of respiration and circulation.  Other criteria are practical in
cases where artificial life-support systems are not utilized.
Even those criteria are indicative of brain death.
"Functioning" is a critical word in the Act.  It expresses
the idea of *purposeful* activity in all parts of the brain, as
distinguished from random activity.  In a dead brain, some mean-
ingless cellular processes, detectable by sensitive monitoring
equipment, could create legal confusion if the word "activity"
were substituted for "functioning."

[States that have adopted modified versions of the proposed

statute are Nevada (1979) and West Virginia (1980; originally en-

acted in 1975, then modeled after the Capron-Kass proposal in

1977.)]

### b.  Uniform Determination of Death Act

The following is the text of the statute approved by the National Conference of Commissioners on Uniform State Laws at its
Annual Conference on July 26-August 1, 1980, by the American Medical Association on October 19, 1980, by the President's Commission on November 7, 1980, and by the American Bar Association on
February 10, 1981 to supersede the existing "model" bills.

*Section 1.* [*Determination of Death.*]  An individual who has
sustained either (1) irreversible cessation of circulatory and
respiratory functions, or (2) irreversible cessation of all functions of the entire brain, including the brain stem, is dead.  A
determination of death must be made in accordance with accepted
medical standards.

*Section 2.* [*Uniformity of Construction and Application.*]
This Act shall be applied and construed to effectuate its general
purpose to make uniform the law with respect to the subject of
this Act among states enacting it.

[States that have adopted modified versions of the proposed

statute are Colorado (1981), the District of Columbia (1981),

Idaho (1981), Mississippi (1981), and Vermont (1981).]

### c.  Statute Proposed by the American Bar Association

The following is the text of the model statute proposed by
the American Bar Association in 1975:

For all legal purposes, a human body with irreversible cessation of total brain function, according to usual and customary
standards of medical practice, shall be considered dead.

[States that have adopted modified versions of the proposed

statute are California (1975), Illinois (1975), Tennessee (1976),

Montana (1977), and Georgia (1979).]

### d.  Capron-Kass Proposal

The following is the modified text of a model bill proposed
in 1972 by Professor Alexander M. Capron and Dr. Leon Kass in an
article in Volume 121 of the *University of Pennsylvania Law Review* at pages 87-118.

A person will be considered dead if in the announced opinion
of a physician, based on ordinary standards of medical practice,
he has experienced an irreversible cessation of respiratory and
circulatory functions, or in the event that artificial means of
support preclude a determination that these functions have
ceased, he has experienced an irreversible cessation of total
brain functions.  Death will have occurred at the time when the
relevant functions ceased.

[States that have adopted modified versions of the proposed

statute are: Alaska (1979), Iowa (1979), Michigan (1979), and

Louisiana (1980), with only minor modifications; and Alabama

(1979), Hawaii (1979), and Texas (1980), with major modifications.

e.  Statute Proposed by the American Medical Association

The following is the amended model state determination of death bill approved at the December 1971 Interim Meeting of the American Medical Association:

*Section 1.*  An individual who has sustained either (1) irreversible cessation of circulatory and respiratory functions, or (2) irreversible cessation of all functions of the entire brain, shall be considered dead.  A determination of death shall be made in accordance with accepted medical standards.

> (COMMENT:  This section is intended to provide a comprehensive statement for determining death in all situations, by clarifying and codifying the common law in this regard. The two bases set forth in the statute are the only medically acceptable bases for determining death, and the statute is therefore all inclusive.  "All functions" of the brain means that purposeful activity of the brain, as distinguished from random activity in the brain, has ceased.  "Entire brain" includes both the brain stem and the neocortex and is meant to distinguish the concept of neocortical death, which is not a valid medical basis for determining death.
>
> It is recognized that physicians may determine death.  It is also recognized that in some jurisdictions non-physicians (i.e. coroners) are empowered to determine death.  It is the intent of this bill to recognize that under accepted medical standards a determination of death based on irreversible cessation of brain function may be made only by a physician.)

*Section 2.*  A physician or any other person authorized by law to determine death who makes such determination in accordance with section 1 is not liable for damages in any civil action or subject to prosecution in any criminal proceeding for his acts or the acts of others based on that determination.

*Section 3.*  Any person who acts in good faith in reliance on a determination of death is not liable for damages in any civil action or subject to prosecution in any criminal proceeding for his act.

> (COMMENT:  While Section 1 is intended to remove legal impediments relating to a declaration of death based on medically accepted principles, sections two and three are intended to remove inhibitions from making a declaration of death based on either of the two standards and also to remove inhibitions of hospital personnel from carrying out the direction of a physician in this regard by removing the threat of liability.  These sections do not absolve from liability a person who acts negligently or contrary to accepted medical standards.)

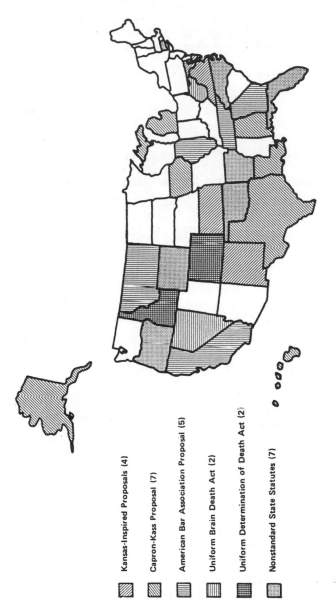

Kansas-Inspired Proposals (4)

Capron-Kass Proposal (7)

American Bar Association Proposal (5)

Uniform Brain Death Act (2)

Uniform Determination of Death Act (2)

Nonstandard State Statutes (7)

State Statutes on the Determination of Death as of July, 1981
(from Defining Death, p. 65).

*Section 4.*   If any provision of this Act is held by a court
to be invalid such invalidity shall not affect the remaining provisions of the Act, and to this end the provisions of this Act
are hereby declared to be severable.

[No states have adopted this proposal.]

      *                           *                           *

NOTE:   Seven states have adopted statutes based not on any

of the preceding models nor on the "Kansas" model.  They are:

Oklahoma (1975), Oregon (1977), North Carolina (1979), Arkansas

(1979), Connecticut (1979), Wyoming (1979), and Florida (1980).

      *                           *                           *

## f.   Uniform Anatomical Gift Act

The Uniform Anatomical Gift Act, proposed by the National Con-

ference of Commissioners on Uniform State Laws, has been adopted

in substantially identical form in all fifty states.

An act authorizing the gift of all or part of a human body
after death for specified purposes.

SECTION 1 [*Definitions*]
    (a) "Bank or storage facility" means a facility licensed, ac-
credited or approved under the laws of any state for storage of
human bodies or parts thereof.
    (b) "Decedent" means a deceased individual and includes a
still-born infant or fetus.
    (c) "Donor" means an individual who makes a gift of all or
part of his body.
    (d) "Hospital" means a hospital licensed, accredited, or ap-
proved under the laws of any state and includes a hospital operated by the United States government, a state, or a subdivision
thereof, although not required to be licensed under state laws.
    (e) "Part" includes organs, tissues, eyes, bones, arteries,
blood, other fluids and other portions of a human body, and "part"
includes "parts."

(f) "Person" means an individual, corporation, government or governmental subdivision or agency, business trust, estate, trust, partnership or association or any other legal entity.

(g) "Physician" or "surgeon" means a physician or surgeon licensed or authorized to practice under the laws of any state.

(h) "State" includes any state, district, commonwealth, territory, insular possession, and any other area subject to the legislative authority of the United States of America.

SECTION 2 [*Persons Who May Execute an Anatomical Gift*]

(a) Any individual of sound mind and 18 years of age or more may give all or any part of his body for any purposes specified in Section 3, the gift to take effect upon death.

(b) Any of the following persons, in order of priority stated, when persons in prior classes are not available at the time of death, and in the absence of actual notice of contrary indications by the decedent, or actual notice of opposition by a member of the same or a prior class, may give all or any part of the decedent's body for any purposes specified in Section 3:

(1) the spouse,
(2) an adult son or daughter,
(3) either parent,
(4) an adult brother or sister,
(5) a guardian of the person of the decedent at the time of his death,
(6) any other person authorized or under obligation to dispose of the body.

(c) If the donee has actual notice of contrary indications by the decedent, or that a gift by a member of a class is opposed by a member of the same or a prior class, the donee shall not accept the gift. The person authorized by subsection (b) may make the gift after death or immediately before death.

(d) A gift of all or part of a body authorizes any examination necessary to assure medical acceptability of the gift for the purposes intended.

(e) The rights of the donee created by the gift are paramount to the rights of others except as provided by Section 7 (d).

SECTION 3 [*Persons Who May Become Donees, and Purposes for Which Anatomical Gifts May be Made*]

(1) any hospital , surgeon, or physician, for medical or dental education, research, advancement of medical or dental science, therapy or transplantation; or

(2) any accredited medical or dental school, college or university for education, research, advancement of medical or dental science or therapy; or

(3) any bank or storage facility, for medical or dental education, research, advancement of medical or dental science, therapy or transplantation; or

(4) any specified individual for therapy or transplantation
needed by him.

SECTION 4 [*Manner of Executing Anatomical Gifts*]
(a) A gift of all or part of the body under Section 2 (a) may
be made by will. The gift becomes effective upon the death of
the testator without waiting for probate. If the will is not pro-
bated, or if it is declared invalid for testamentary purposes,
the gift, to the extent that it has been acted upon in good faith,
is nevertheless valid and effective.
(b) A gift of all or part of the body under Section 2 (a) may
also be made by document other than a will. The gift becomes effective upon the death of the donor. The document, which may be
a card designed to be carried on the person, must be signed by
the donor, in the presence of 2 witnesses who must sign the document in his presence. If the donor cannot sign, the document may
be signed for him at his direction and in his presence, and in
the presence of 2 witnesses who must sign the document in his presence. Delivery of the document of gift during the donor's lifetime is not necessary to make the gift valid.
(c) The gift may be made to a specified donee or without
specifying a donee. If the latter, the gift may be accepted by
the attending physician as donee upon or following death. If the
gift is made to a specified donee who is not available at the
time and place of death, the attending physician upon or following death, in the absence of any expressed indication that the
donor desired otherwise, may accept the gift as donee. The physician who becomes a donee under this subsection shall not participate in the procedures for removing or transplanting a part.
(d) Notwithstanding Section 7 (b), the donor may designate
in his will, card or other document of gift the surgeon or physician to carry out the appropriate procedures. In the absence of
a designation, or if the designee is not available, the donee or
other person authorized to accept the gift may employ or authorize any surgeon or physician for the purpose.
(e) Any gift by a person designated in Section 2 (b) shall be
made by a document signed by him, or made by his telegraphic, recorded telephonic or other recorded message.

SECTION 5 [*Delivery of Document of Gift*] If the gift is
made by the donor to a specified donee, the will, card or other
document, or an executed copy thereof, may be delivered to the
donee to expedite the appropriate procedures immediately after
death, but delivery is not necessary to the validity of the gift.
The will, card or other document, or an executed copy thereof,
may be deposited in any hospital, bank or storage facility or
registry office that accepts them for safekeeping or for facil-
itation of procedures after death. On request of any interested
party upon or after the donor's death, the person in possession
shall produce the document for examination.

SECTION 6 [*Amendment or Revocation of the Gift*]

(a) If the will, card or other document or executed copy thereof, has been delivered to a specific donee, the donor may amend or revoke the gift by:

    (1) the execution and delivery to the donee of a signed statement, or

    (2) an oral statement made in the presence of 2 persons and communicated to the donee, or

    (3) a statement during a terminal illness or injury addressed to an attending physician and communicated to the donee, or

    (4) a signed card or document found on his person or in his effects.

(b) Any document of gift which has not been delivered to the donee may be revoked by the donor in the manner set out in subsection (a) or by destruction, cancellation, or mutilation of the document and all executed copies thereof.

(c) Any gift made by a will may also be amended or revoked in the manner provided for amendment or revocation of wills, or as provided in subsection.(a).

SECTION 7 [*Rights and Duties at Death*]

(a) The donee may accept or reject the gift. If the donee accepts a gift of the entire body, he may, subject to the terms of the gift, authorize embalming and the use of the body in funeral services. If the gift is of a part of the body, the donee, upon the death of the donor and prior to embalming, shall cause the part to be removed without unnecessary mutilation. After removal of the part, custody of the remainder of the body vests in the surviving spouse, next of kin or other persons under obligation to dispose of the body.

(b) The time of death shall be determined by a physician who attends the donor at his death, or, if none, the physician who certifies the death. This physician shall not participate in the procedures for removing or transplanting a part.

(c) A person who acts in good faith in accord with the terms of this Act, or under the anatomical gift laws of another state [or a foreign country] is not liable for damages in any civil action or subject to prosecution in any criminal proceeding for his act.

(d) The provisions of this Act are subject to the laws of this state prescribing powers and duties with respect to autopsies.

SECTION 8 [*Uniformity of Interpretation*] This Act shall be so construed as to effectuate its general purpose to make uniform the law of those states which enact it.

SECTION 9 [*Short Title*] This Act may be cited as the Uniform Anatomical Gift Act.

SECTION 10 [*Repeal*] The following acts and parts of acts are repealed:
        (1)
        (2)
        (3)

SECTION 11 [*Time of Taking Effect*] This Act shall take effect . . .

## IV.  INFORMED CONSENT


### A.  Consent to Therapy

To date, there are approximately 225 appellate decisions
dealing with the issue of informed consent.  Fewer than 25% (50
cases) mention the basis on which the court found or failed to
find informed consent necessary.  Of those that do give a basis,
more than half rely on the patient's right of self-determination.  Most of the other cases rely on the fiduciary qualities
inherent in the doctor-patient relationship.  Representative
cases follow.


### 1.  Judicial Decisions

#### a. *Canterbury v. Spence*, 464 F.2d 772 (D.C. Cir. 1972)

> The record we review tells a depressing tale.  A
> youth troubled only by back pain submitted to an operation with-
> out being informed of a risk of paralysis incidental thereto.
> A day after the operation he fell from his hospital bed after
> having been left without assistance while voiding.  A few hours
> after the fall, the lower half of his body was paralyzed, and
> he had to be operated on again.  Despite extensive medical care,
> he has never been what he was before.  Instead of the back pain,
> even years later, he hobbled about on crutches, a victim of
> paralysis of the bowels and urinary incontinence.  In a very
> real sense this lawsuit is an understandable search for rea-
> sons.
> At the time of the events which gave rise to this
> litigation, appellant was nineteen years of age, a clerk-typist

employed by the Federal Bureau of Investigation.  In December, 1958, he began to experience severe pain between his shoulder blades.  He consulted two general practitioners, but the medications they prescribed failed to eliminate the pain.  Thereafter, appellant secured an appointment with Dr. Spence, who is a neurosurgeon.

Dr. Spence examined appellant in his office at some length but found nothing amiss.  On Dr. Spence's advice appellant was x-rayed, but the films did not identify any abnormality.  Dr. Spence then recommended that appellant undergo a myelogram--a procedure in which dye is injected into the spinal column and traced to find evidence of disease or other disorder--at the Washington Hospital Center.

Appellant entered the hospital on February 4, 1959. The myelogram revealed a "filling defect" in the region of the fourth thoracic vertebra.  Since a myelogram often does not more than pinpoint the location of an aberration, surgery may be necessary to discover the cause.  Dr. Spence told appellant that he would have to undergo a laminectomy--the excision of the posterior arch of the vertebra--to correct what he suspected was a ruptured disc.  Appellant did not raise any objection to the proposed operation nor did he probe into its exact nature.

Appellant explained to Dr. Spence that his mother was a widow of slender financial means living in Cyclone, West Virginia, and that she could be reached through a neighbor's telephone.  Appellant called his mother the day after the myelogram was performed and, failing to contact her, left Dr. Spence"s telephone number with the neighbor.  When Mrs. Canterbury returned the call, Dr. Spence told her that the surgery was occasioned by a suspected ruptured disc.  Mrs. Canterbury then asked if the recommended operation was serious and Dr. Spence replied "not anymore than any other operation."  He added that he knew Mrs. Canterbury was not well off and that her presence in Washington would not be necessary.  The testimony is contradictory as to whether during the course of the conversation Mrs. Canterbury expressed her consent to the operation. Appellant himself apparently did not converse again with Dr. Spence prior to the operation.

Dr. Spence performed the laminectomy on February 11 at the Washington Hospital Center.  Mrs. Canterbury traveled to Washington, arriving on that date but after the operation was over, and signed a consent form at the hospital.  The laminectomy revealed several anomalies: a spinal cord that was swollen and unable to pulsate, an accumulation of large tortuous and dilated veins, and a complete absence of epidural fat which normally surrounds the spine.  A thin hypodermic needle was inserted into the spinal cord to aspirate any cysts which might have been present, but no fluid emerged.  In suturing the wound,

Dr. Spence attempted to relieve the pressure on the spinal cord
by enlarging the dura--the outer protective wall of the spinal
cord--at the area of swelling.

For approximately the first day after the operation
appellant recuperated normally, but then suffered a fall and
an almost immediate setback. Since there is some conflict as
to precisely when or why appellant fell, we reconstruct the
events from the evidence most favorable to him. Dr. Spence
left orders that appellant was to remain in bed during the
process of voiding. These orders were changed to direct that
voiding be done out of bed, and the jury could find that the
change was made by hospital personnel. Just prior to the fall,
appellant summoned a nurse and was given a receptacle for use
in voiding, but was then left unattended. Appellant testified
that during the course of the endeavor he slipped off the side
of the bed, and that there was no one to assist him, or side
rail to prevent the fall.

Several hours later, appellant began to complain
that he could not move his legs and that he was having trouble
breathing; paralysis seems to have been virtually total from
the waist down. Dr. Spence was notified on the night of
February 12, and he rushed to the hospital. Mrs. Canterbury
signed another consent form and appellant was again taken into
the operating room. The surgical wound was reopened and Dr.
Spence created a gusset to allow the spinal cord greater room
in which to pulsate.

Appellant's control over his muscles improved somewhat after the second operation but he was unable to void properly. As a result of this condition, he came under the care of
a urologist while still in the hospital. In April, following
a cystoscopic examination, appellant was operated on for removal of bladder stones, and in May was released from the hospital. He reentered the hospital the following August for a
10-day period, apparently because of his urologic problems. For
several years after his discharge he was under the care of
several specialists, and at all times was under the care of a
urologist. At the time of the trial in April, 1968, appellant
required crutches to walk, still suffered from urinal incon-
tinence and paralysis of the bowels, and wore a penile clamp.

Suits charging failure by a physician adequately to
disclose the risks and alternatives of proposed treatment are
not innovations in American law. They date back a good half-
century, and in the last decade they have multiplied rapidly.
There is, nonetheless, disagreement among the courts and the
commentators on many major questions, and there is no precedent
of our own directly in point. For the tools enabling resolution of the issues on this appeal, we are forced to begin at
first principles.

The root premise is the concept, fundamental in
American jurisprudence, that "[e]very human being of adult years
and sound mind has a right to determine what shall be done with
his own body . . . ." True consent to what happens to one's
self is the informed exercise of a choice, and that entails an
opportunity to evaluate knowledgeably the options available and
the risks attendant upon each. The average patient has little
or no understanding of the medical arts, and ordinarily has
only his physician to whom he can look for enlightenment with
which to reach an intelligent decision. From these almost axio-
matic considerations springs the need, and in turn the requirement, of a reasonable divulgence by physician to patient to
make such a decision possible.

A physician is under a duty to treat his patient
skillfully but proficiency in diagnosis and therapy is not the
full measure of his responsibility. The cases demonstrate that
the physician is under an obligation to communicate specific
information to the patient when the exigencies of reasonable
care call for it. Due care may require a physician perceiving
symptoms of bodily abnormality to alert the patient to the condition. It may call upon the physician confronting an ailment
which does not respond to his ministrations to inform the
patient thereof. It may command the physician to instruct the
patient as to any limitations to be presently observed for his
own welfare, and as to any precautionary thereapy he should
seek in the future. It may oblige the physician to advise the
patient of the need for or desirability of any alternative
treatment promising greater benefit than that being pursued.
Just as plainly, due care normally demands that the physician
warn the patient of any risks to his well-being which contemplated thereapy may involve.

The contest in which the duty of rish-disclosure
arises is invariably the occasion for decision as to whether a
particular treatment procedure is to be undertaken. To the
physician, whose training enables a self-satisfying evaluation,
the answer may seem clear, but it is the prerogative of the
patient, not the physician, to determine for himself the direction in which his interests seem to lie. To enable the
patient to chart his course understandably, some familiarity
with the therapeutic alternatives and their hazards becomes
essential.

A reasonable revelation in these respects is not
only a necessity but, as we see it, is as much a matter of the
physician's duty. It is a duty to warn of the dangers lurking
in the proposed treatment, and that is surely a facet of due
care. It is, too, a duty to impart information which the patient has every right to expect. The patient's reliance upon
the physician is a trust of the kind which traditionally has

exacted obligations beyond those associated with armslength transactions.  His dependence upon the physician for information affecting his well-being, in terms of contemplated treatment, is well-nigh abject.  As earlier noted, long before the instant litigation arose, courts had recognized that the physician had the responsibility of satisfying the vital informational needs of the patient.  More recently, we ourselves have found "in the fiducial qualities of [the physician-patient] relationship the physician's duty to reveal to the patient that which in his best interests it is important that he should know."  We now find, as a part of the physician's overall obligation to the patient, a similar duty of reasonable disclosure of the choices with respect to proposed therapy and the dangers inherently and potentially involved.

This disclosure requirement, on analysis, reflects much more of a change in doctrinal emphasis than a substantive addition to malpractice law.  It is well established that the physician must seek and secure his patient's consent before commencing an operation or other course of treatment.  It is also clear that the consent, to be efficacious, must be free from imposition upon the patient.  It is the settled rule that therapy not authorized by the patient may amount to a tort--a common law battery--by the physician.  And it is evident that it is normally impossible to obtain a consent worthy of the name unless the physician first elucidates the options and the perils for the patient's effication.  Thus the physician has long borne a duty, on pain of liability for unauthorized treatment, to make adequate disclosure to the patient.  The evolution of the obligation to communicate for the patient's benefit as well as the physician's protection has hardly involved an extraordinary restructuring of the law.

Duty to disclose has gained recognition in a large number of American jurisdictions, but more largely on a different rationale.  The majority of courts dealing with the problem have made the duty depend on whether it was the custom of physicians practicing in the community to make the particular disclosure to the patient.  If so, the physician may be held liable for an unreasonable and injurious failure to divulge, but there can be no recovery unless the omission forsakes a practice prevalent in the profession.  We agree that the physician's noncompliance with a professional custom to reveal, like any other departure from prevailing medical practice, may give rise to liability to the patient.  We do not agree that the patient's cause of action is dependent upon the existence and nonperformance of a relevant professional tradition . . . to bind the disclosure obligation to medical usage is to arrogate the decision on revelation to the physician alone.  Respect for the patient's right of self-determination on particular therapy

demands a standard set by law for physicians rather than one
which physicians may or may not impose upon themselves . . . .
        Once the circumstances give rise to a duty on the
physician's part to inform his patient, the next inquiry is the
scope of the disclosure the physician is legally obliged to
make . . . .
        In our view, the patient's right of self-decision
shapes the boundaries of the duty to reveal. That right can be
effectively exercised only if the patient possesses enough information to enable an intelligent choice. The scope of the
physician's communications to the patient, then, must be measured by the patient's need, and that need is the information
material to the decision. Thus the test for determining whether
a particular peril must be divulged is its materiality to the
patient's decision: all risks potentially affecting the decision must be unmasked. And to safeguard the patient's interest in achieving his own determination on treatment, the law
must itself set the standard for adequate disclosure.
        Optimally, for the patient, exposure of a risk would
be mandatory whenever the patient would deem it significant to
his decision, either singly or in combination with other risks.
Such a requirement, however, would summon the physician to
second-guess the patient, whose ideas on materiality could
hardly be known to the physician. That would make an undue
demand upon medical practitioners whose conduct, like that of
others, is to be measured in terms of reasonableness . . . .
        . . . The scope of the standard is not subjective
as to either the physician or the patient; it remains objective
with due regard for the patient's informational needs and with
suitable leeway for the physician's situation. In broad outline, we agree that "[a] risk is thus material when a reasonable
person, in what the physician knows or should know to be the
patient's position, would be likely to attach significance to
the risk or cluster of risks in deciding whether or not to
forego the proposed therapy.
        The topics importantly demanding a communication of
information are the inherent and potential hazards of the proposed treatment, the alternatives to that treatment, if any,
and the results likely if the patient remains untreated. The
factors contributing significance to the dangerousness of a
medical technique are, of course, the incidence of injury and
the degree of the harm threatened. A very small chance of
death or serious disablement may well be significant; a potential disability which dramatically outweighs the potential
benefit of the therapy or the detriments of the existing malady
may summons discussion with the patient.
        There is no bright line separating the significant
from the insignificant; the answer in any case must abide a

rule of reason.  Some dangers--infection, for example--are inherent in any operation; there is no obligation to communicate
those of which persons of average sophistication are aware.
Even more clearly, the physician bears no responsibility for
discussion of hazards the patient has already discovered, or
those having no apparent materiality to patients' decision on
therapy.  The disclosure doctrine, like others marking lines
between permissible and impermissible behavior in medical practice, is in essence a requirement of conduct prudent under the
circumstances.  Whenever nondisclosure of particular risk information is open to debate by reasonable-minded men, the issue
is for the finder of the facts.
        Two exceptions to the general rule of disclosure
have been noted by the courts.  Each is in the nature of a physician's privilege not to disclose, and the reasoning underlying them is appealing.  Each, indeed, is but a recognition that,
as important as is the patient's right to know, it is greatly
outweighed by the magnitudinous circumstances giving rise to
the privilege.  The first comes into play when the patient is
unconscious or otherwise incapable of consenting, and harm from
a failure to treat is imminent and outweighs any harm threatened by the proposed treatment.  When a genuine emergency of
that sort arises, it is settled that the impracticality of con-
ferring with the patient dispenses with need for it.  Even in
situations of that character the physician should, as current
law requires, attempt to secure a relative's consent if possible.
But if time is too short to accommodate discussion, obviously
the physician should proceed with the treatment.
        The second exception obtains when risk-disclosure
poses such a threat of detriment to the patient as to become
unfeasible or contraindicated from a medical point of view.  It
is recognized that patients occasionally become so ill or emotionally distraught on disclosure as to foreclose a rational
decision, or perhaps even pose psychological damage to the patient.  Where that is so, the cases have generally held that
the physician is armed with a privilege to keep the information
from the patient, and we think it clear that portents of that
type may justify the physician in action he deems medically
warranted.  The critical inquiry is whether the physician re-
sponded to a sound medical judgement that communication of the
risk information would present a threat to the patient's well-
being.


        b.  *Cobbs v. Grant*, 104 Cal. 505, 502 P.2d 4 (1972)

        The plaintiff, a middle-aged gentleman, underwent

surgery to correct a duodenal ulcer.  He was not informed of any possible complications.  Following surgery he was readmitted to the hospital with internal bleeding (the risk of this occurring after surgery is about 5%), and a splenectomy was performed to stop it.  A month later he suffered severe stomach pains, which turned out to be a new ulcer, and much of his stomach had to be surgically removed.  This risk was also predictable.

The surgeon testified that it was not customary to inform patients of such risks.  The court, however, found that physicians had a fiduciary duty to their patients to make certain disclosures before they performed risky procedures on them:

> . . . as an integral part of the physician's overall obligation to the patient there is a duty of reasonable disclosure of the available choices with respect to proposed therapy and of the dangers inherently and potentially involved in each.

Specifically, the court required disclosure of the following:

1. a description of the proposed treatment;

2. alternatives to the proposed treatment;

3. inherent risks of death or serious bodily injury in the proposed treatment and the alternatives;

4. problems of recuperation that are anticipated; and

5. any additional information other physicians would disclose under similar circumstances.

The California Supreme Court also summarized the major
exceptions to the disclosure requirements as follows:

1. in an emergency;

2. if the patient does not want to be informed;

3. if the procedure is simple, and the danger is remote
   and commonly appreciated as remote; and

4. if in the physician's judgment it is not in the patient's best interest to know (e.g., when the information would so seriously upset the patient that he could
   not rationally make a decision).

   c.  *Cox v. Haworth*, S.E. (N.C. 1981)

         In this case, a North Carolina appellate court
found that a hospital had no duty to obtain informed consent
from a plaintiff who had undergone surgery in the hospital.  Mr.
Alfred Cox, the plaintiff, received a myelogram from a private
physician in High Point Memorial Hospital.  The physician, Dr.
Haworth, neglected to remove all the dye injected into Mr. Cox
during the myelogram.  As a result, Mr. Cox suffered severe and
incapacitating pain and scarring of the spinal cord.  The
plaintiff sued the hospital, under theories of agency, corpor-
ate negligence, and battery, for failing to give him informed
consent before the procedure.

         The court rejected Mr. Cox's arguments, finding
that the hospital had no duty to obtain informed consent when

the patient is under the care of a private physician.  In such
cases, the hospital's role is only to provide support personnel
and facilities for the operation.  The court noted that Cox had
not alleged hospital negligence in selecting or referring private physicians, in staffing support personnel, or in administering drugs.  While hospitals do have a variety of duties relating to patient care, including the duty to inspect equipment
and promulgate safety rules, the plaintiff had not alleged
breach of any recognized hospital duties.  Under these circumstances, the hospital was not liable for the failure of a private physician to obtain informed consent prior to operating
within the hospital.

    2.   <u>Statutes</u>

       In response to the medical malpractice insurance crisis,
25 states enacted informed consent legislation between 1975 and
1977;  Alaska, Colorado, Delaware, Florida, Hawaii, Idaho,
Iowa, Kentucky, Louisiana, Maine, Nebraska, Nevada, New Hamp-
shire, New York, North Carolina, North Dakota, Ohio, Oregon,
Pennsylvania, Rhode Island, Tennessee, Texas, Utah, Vermont,
and Washington.  All were designed either to define or restrict
the application of the doctrine of informed consent.  Most of
them attempted to make it more difficult for a plaintiff to
successfully sue a physician who failed to obtain informed
consent.

        Statutes in nine states, for example, provide that a
patient's signature on a consent form shall be conclusive evidence that the information was provided to the patient and that
the consent was valid.  Florida's statute provides that the
signed consent shall be "conclusively presumed to be valid consent.  This presumption "may be rebutted if there was a *fraudu-
lent misrepresentation of a material fact* in obtaining the signature" (emphasis supplied in this and the three quotes that
follow).  Idaho's statute likewise provides that "such written
consent, in the absence of convincing proof that it was *secured
maliciously or by fraud,* is presumed to be valid . . . and the
advice and disclosures of the attending physician or dentist, as
well as the *level of informed awareness* of the giver of such
consent, shall be presumed sufficient.  In Iowa:

> A consent in writing to any medical or surgical pro-
> cedure or course of procedures *in patient care* which
> meets the requirements of this section *shall create a
> presumption* that informed consent was given.

And in Ohio:

> Written consent to a surgical or medical procedure or
> course of procedures shall, to the extent that it ful-
> fills . . . [certain requirements] *be presumed to be
> valid and effective,* in the absence of proof by a pre-
> ponderance of the evidence that the person who sought
> such consent was *not acting in good faith,* or that the
> execution of the consent was induced by *fraudulent
> misrepresentation of material facts,* or that the person
> executing the consent was *not able to communicate ef-
> fectively* in spoken or written *English* or any other
> language in which the consent is written.

        In Iowa and Ohio, statutes also contain lists of the
types of risks that require disclosure by physicians.  The
language of each is set forth because it indicates the types of
risks a legislature (as opposed to a court) finds to be significant to patients in the therapeutic setting.  The lists are
identical; both statutes require disclosure of the following
risks: "death, brain damage, quadriplegia, paraplegia, the loss
of function of any organ or limb, or disfiguring scars . . .
with the probability of each such risk if reasonably determin-
able.  Statutes in eight other states are similar to New York's,
in which the physician is required to disclose only those "risks
and benefits involved as a reasonable medical practitioner
under similar circumstances would have disclosed . . ."  Five
other states--Colorado, Utah, Nevada, Alaska, and Idaho--(in

addition to Ohio and Iowa) adopt their own definitions of informed consent, while Pennsylvania and Washington base disclosure on the "risks and alternatives to treatment or diagnosis
that a reasonable patient would consider material to the decision whether or not to undergo treatment or diagnosis."
          Ohio goes one step further, and is the only state legis-
lature which sets forth a model consent form in its statute,
providing that if this form is properly used, consent shall be
presumed to be valid.  Because of its uniqueness, the entire
text of the form [Ohio Rev. Code Ann: sec. 2317.54] is set forth
here:

CONSENT FOR MEDICAL PROCEDURE AND ACKNOWLEDGEMENT OF RECEIPT OF
RISK INFORMATION

State law requires us to obtain your consent to your contemplated surgery or other medical procedure.  What you are being
asked to sign is simply a confirmation that we have discussed
your contemplated operation or medical procedure and that we
have given you sufficient information upon which to make a decision whether to have the operation or medical procedure and
any choice as to the type of operation or medical procedure of
your own free will.  We have already discussed with you the
common problems or undesired results that sometimes occur.  We
wish to inform you, not to alarm you.  If you wish, however, we
can go into more elaborate details or more unlikely problems.
If you do not, that is also your privilege.  Please read the
form carefully and check the appropriate boxes.  Ask about anything that you do not understand.  We will be pleased to explain it.  I hereby authorize and direct _____, with
associate or assistants of his choice to perform the following
surgical, diagnostic, or medical procedure on _____,
my _____, as we have agreed upon.
(relationship)

---

I further authorize the doctors to perform any other procedure
that in their judgment is advisable for my well being.  Details
of this operation have been explained to me.  Alternative methods of treatment, if any, have also been explained to me as
have the advantages and disadvantages of each.  I am advised
that though good results are expected, the possibility and
nature of complications cannot be accurately anticipated and
that therefore there can be no guarantee as expressed or implied either as to the result of surgery or as to cure.

Degree and kind of risks known to be associated with this procedure, including anesthesia; each marked box indicates some risks that are associated with this procedure:

Comments

☐ Death
☐ Brain Damage
☐ Quadriplegia (paralysis of all arms and legs)
☐ Paraplegia (paralysis of both legs)
☐ Loss of organ
☐ Loss of an arm or leg
☐ Loss of function of organ
☐ Loss of function of an arm or leg
☐ Disfiguring scars

The doctor has explained to me the most likely complications or undesired results that might occur in this operation or medical procedure and I understand them. The doctor has offered to detail the less likely complications of [sic] undesired results which, even if rare, could occur.

_____ I do _____ I do not wish to have a full description of all the possible complications given to me.

I hereby authorize and direct the above named physician with associates or assistants to provide such additional services as they might deem reasonable and necessary including, but not limited to, the administration of any anesthetic agent, or the services of the X-ray department or laboratories, and I hereby consent thereto.

I hereby state that I have read and understand this consent and that all blanks were filled in prior to my signature.

Date: _____ Time _____ a.m.p.m.

Signature of Patient _____
Signature of Relative (where required) _____
Witness _____

I certify that I have personally completed all blanks in this form and explained them to the patient or his representative before requesting the patient or his representative to sign it.

_____(signature of named physician)

B.    Consent to Experimentation


1. Codes


a.    The Nuremberg Code (1946)

The Nuremberg Code was formulated by a panel of

three United States judges in the trial of 23 German physicians

charged after World War Ii with "war crimes and crimes against

humanity" for their experiments with prisoners of war and ci-

vilians.   It was adopted by the General Assembly of the United

Nations on December 11, 1946.

1.  The voluntary consent of the human subject is absolutely essential.  This means that the person involved
should have legal capacity to give consent; should be so
situated as to be able to exercise free power of choice,
without the intervention of any element of force, fraud,
deceit, duress, overreaching, or other ulterior form of
constraint or coercion; and should have sufficient knowledge and comprehension of the elements of the subject
matter involved as to enable him to make an understanding
and enlightened decision.  This latter element requires
that before the acceptance of an affirmative decision by
the experimental subject there should be made known to him
the nature, duration, and purpose of the experiment; the
method and means by which it is to be conducted; all inconveniences and hazards reasonably to be expected; and
the effects upon his health or person which may possibly
come from his participation in the experiments.
The duty and responsibility for ascertaining the
quality of the consent rests upon each individual who ini-
tiates, directs or engages in the experiment.  It is a
personal duty and responsibility which may not be delegated to another with impunity.
2.  The experiment should be such as to yield fruitful
results for the good of society, unprocurable by other
methods or means of study, and not random and unnecessary
in nature.

3. The experiment should be so designed and based on the results of animal experimentation and a knowledge of the natural history of the disease or other problem under study that the anticipated results [will] justify the performance of the experiment.

4. The experiment should be so conducted as to avoid all unnecessary physical and mental suffering and injury.

5. No experiment should be conducted where there is an a priori reason to believe that death or disabling injury will occur; except, perhaps, in those experiments where the experimental physicians also serve as subjects.

6. The degree of risk to be taken should never exceed that determined by the humanitarian importance of the problem to be solved by the experiment.

7. Proper preparations should be made and adequate facilities provided to protect the experimental subject against even remote possibilities of injury, disability, or death.

8. The experiment should be conducted only by scientifically qualified persons. The highest degree of skill and care should be required through all stages of the experiment of those who conduct or engage in the experiment.

9. During the course of the experiment the human subject should be at liberty to bring the experiment to an end if he has reached the physical or mental state where continuation of the experiment seems to him to be impossible.

10. During the course of the experiment the scientist in charge must be prepared to terminate the experiment at any stage, if he has probable cause to believe, in the exercise of good faith, superior skill and careful judgment required of him that a continuation of the experiment is likely to result in injury, disability, or death to the experimental subject.

Of the ten principles which have been enumerated our judicial concern, of course, is with those requirements which are purely legal in nature--or which at least are so clearly related to matters legal that they assist us in determining criminal culpability and punishment. To go beyond that point would lead us into a field that would be beyond our sphere of competence. However, the point need not be labored. We find from the evidence that in the medical experiments which have been proved, these ten principles were much more frequently honored in their breach than in their observance. Many of the concentration camp inmates who were the victims of these atrocities were citizens of countries other than the German Reich. They were non-German nationals, including Jews and "asocial persons," both prisoners of war and civilians, who had been imprisoned and forced to submit to these tortures and barbarities without

so much as a semblance of trial.  In every single instance ap-
pearing in the record, subjects were used who did not consent
to the experiments; indeed, as to some of the experiments, it
is not even contended by the defendants that the subjects oc-
cupied the status of volunteers.  In no case was the experimental subject at liberty of his own free choice to withdraw
from any experiment.  In many cases experiments were performed
by unqualified persons; were conducted at random for  no adequate scientific reason, and under revolting physical conditions.  All of the experiments were conducted with unnecessary
suffering and injury and but very little, if any, precautions
were taken to protect or safeguard the human subjects from the
possibilities of injury, disability, or death.  In every one of
the experiments the subjects experienced extreme pain or tor-
ture, and in most of them they suffered permanent injury, mutilation, or death, either as a direct result of the experiments
or because of lack of adequate follow-up care.
     Obviously all of these experiments involving brutalities,
tortures, disabling injury, and death were performed in complete
disregard of international conventions, the laws and customs of
war, the general principles of criminal law as derived from the
criminal laws of all civilized nations, and Control Council Law
No. 10.  Manifestly human experiments under such conditions are
contrary to "the principles of the law of nations as they result from the usages established among civilized peoples, from
the laws of humanity, and from the dictates of public conscience."


     b.   Declaration of Helsinki (1964, 1975)

     Adopted by the 18th World Medical Assembly, Hel-

sinki, Finland, 1964, and Revised by the 29th World Medical

Assembly, Tokyo, Japan, 1975, the Declaration of Helsinki gave

"recommendations guiding medical doctors in biomedical research

involving human subjects."

                        *Introduction*

     It is the mission of the medical doctor to safeguard the
health of the people.  His or her knowledge and conscience are
dedicated to the fulfillment of this mission.
     The Declaration of Geneva of the World Medical Association
binds the doctor with the world, "The health of my patient will

be my first consideration," and the International Code of Medical Ethics declares that, "Any act or advice which could weaken physical or mental resistance of a human being may be used only in his interest."

The purpose of biomedical research involving human subjects must be to improve diagnostic, therapeutic and prophylactic procedures and the understanding of the aetiology and pathogenesis of disease.

In current medical practice most diagnostic, therapeutic or prophylactic procedures involve hazards. This applies *a fortiori* to biomedical research.

Medical progress is based on research which ultimately must rest in part on experimentation involving human subjects.

In the field of biomedical research a fundamental distinction must be recognized between medical research in which the aim is essentially diagnostic or therapeutic for a patient, and medical research, the essential object of which is purely scientific and without direct diagnostic or therapeutic value to the person subjected to the research.

Special caution must be exercised in the conduct of research which may affect the environment, and the welfare of animals used for research must be respected.

Because it is essential that the results of laboratory experiments be applied to human beings to further scientific knowledge and to help suffering humanity, The World Medical Association has prepared the following recommendations as a guide to every doctor in biomedical research involving human subjects. They should be kept under review in the future. It must be stressed that the standards as drafted are only a guide to physicians all over the world. Doctors are not relieved from criminal, civil and ethical responsibilities under the laws of their own countries.

## I.  *Basic Principles*

1. Biomedical research involving human subjects must conform to generally accepted scientific principles and should be based on adequately performed laboratory and animal experimentation and on a thorough knowledge of the scientific literature.

2. The design and performance of each experimental procedure involving human subjects should be clearly formulated in an experimental protocol which should be transmitted to a specially appointed independent committee for consideration, comment and guidance.

3. Biomedical research involving human subjects should be conducted only by scientifically qualified persons and under the supervision of a clinically competent medical person. The

responsibility for the human subject must always rest with a medically qualified person and never rest on the subject of the research, even though the subject has given his or her consent.

4. Biomedical research involving human subjects cannot legitimately be carried out unless the importance of the objective is in proportion to the inherent risk to the subject.

5. Every biomedical research project involving human subjects should be preceded by careful assessment of predictable risks in comparison with forseeable benefits to the subject or to others. Concern for the interests of the subject must always prevail over the interest of science and society.

6. The right of the research subject to safeguard his or her integrity must always be respected. Every precaution should be taken to respect the privacy of the subject and to minimize the impact of the study on the subject's physical and mental integrity and on the personality of the subject.

7. Doctors should abstain from engaging in research projects involving human subjects unless they are satisfied that the hazards involved are believed to be predictable. Doctors should cease any investigation if the hazards are found to outweigh the potential benefits.

8. In publication of the results of his or her research, the doctor is obliged to preserve the accuracy of the results. Reports of experimentation not in accordance with the principles laid down in this Declaration should not be accepted for publication.

9. In any research on human beings, each potential subject must be adequately informed of the aims, methods, anticipated benefits and potential hazards of the study and the discomfort it may entail. He or she should be informed that he or she is at liberty to abstain from participation in the study and that he or she is free to withdraw his or her consent to participation at any time. The doctor should then obtain the subject's freely-given informed consent, preferably in writing.

10. When obtaining informed consent for the research project the doctor should be particularly cautious if the subject is in a dependent relationship to him or her or may consent under duress. In that case the informed consent should be obtained by a doctor who is not engaged in the investigation and who is completely independent of this official relationship.

11. In case of legal incompetence, informed consent should be obtained from the legal guardian in accordance with national legislation. Where physical or mental incapacity makes it impossible to obtain informed consent, or when the subject is a minor, permission from the responsible relative replaces that of the subject in accordance with national legislation.

12. The research protocol should always contain a statement of the ethical considerations involved and should indicate that

the principles enunciated in the present Declaration are
complied with.

## II.  *Medical Research Combined with Professional Care*
### *(Clinical Research)*

1. In the treatment of the sick person, the doctor must be
free to use a new diagnostic and therapeutic measure, if in his
or her judgment it offers hope of saving life, reestablishing
health or alleviating suffering.
2. The potential benefits, hazards and discomfort of a new
method should be weighed against the advantages of the best current diagnostic and therapeutic methods.
3. In any medical study, every patient--including those of
a control group, if any--should be assured of the best proven
diagnostic and therapeutic method.
4. The refusal of the patient to participate in a study
must never interfere with the doctor-patient relationship.
5. If the doctor considers it essential not to obtain informed consent, the specific reasons for this proposal should
be stated in the experimental protocol for transmission to the
independent committee (I,2).
6. The doctor can combine medical research with professional care, the objective being the acquisition of new medical
knowledge, only to the extent that medical research is justified
by its potential diagnostic or therapeutic value for the patient.

In 1975 Part II, paragraph 6 was amended as follows:

2. The doctor can combine clinical research with professional care, the objective being the acquisition of new medical
knowledge, only to the extent that clinical research is justified by its therapeutic value for the patient.

## III. *Non-therapeutic Biomedical Research Involving Human Subjects*
### *(Non-clinical biomedical research)*

1. In the purely scientific application of medical research
carried out on a human being, it is the duty of the duty to remain the protector of the life and health of that person on whom
biomedical research is being carried out.
2. The subjects should be volunteers--either healthy persons or patients for whom the experimental design is not related to the patient's illness.
3. The investigator or the investigating team should discontinue the research if in his/her or their judgment it may, if
continued, be harmful to the individual.

4. In research on man, the interest of science and society should never take precedence over considerations related to the wellbeing of the subject.

The amendments of Part III follow:

### III.  *Non-therapeutic Clinical Research*

1.  In the purely scientific application of clinical research carried out on a human being it is the duty of the doctor to remain the protector of the life and health of that person on whom clinical research is being carried out.

2.  The nature, the purpose, and the risk of clinical research must be explained to the subject by the doctor.

3a. Clinical research on a human being cannot be undertaken without his free consent, after he has been fully informed; if he is legally incompetent the consent of the legal guardian should be procured.

3b. The subject of clinical research should be in such a mental, physical, and legal state as to be able to exercise fully his power of choice.

3c. Consent should as a rule be obtained in writing. However, the responsibility for clinical research always remains with the research worker; it never falls on the subject, even after consent is obtained.

4a. The investigator must respect the right of each individual to safeguard his personal integrity, especially if the subject is in a dependent relationship to the investigator.

4b. At any time during the course of clinical research the subject or his guardian should be free to withdraw permission for research to be continued.  The investigator or the investigating team should discontinue the research if in his or their judgment it may, if continued, be harmful to the individual.


2.  Judicial Decisions


a. *Fiorentino v. Wenger*, 26 App. Div. 2d 696, 272 N.Y.S.2d 557 (1966)

The defendant surgeon had developed his own method for treating scoliosis (curvature of the spine) and was the only person in the country using it.  He had used it 35 times, 5 times with "unexpected and untoward results," including one case of complete paralysis.  The plaintiff's 14-year-old son underwent his operation, which involved the insertion of a steel bar or "spinal jack" screwed into the vertebral column. He died from an "exsanguinating hemorrhage" as a result. The issue in the lawsuit was lack of informed consent. The court found that because the procedure was "novel and unorthodox" the physician was obligated to make a disclosure to the parents concerning the "risks incident to or possible in its use." The lower court also held the hospital responsible for the failure to disclose, but this portion of the decision was reversed on appeal.

b. *Karp v. Cooley*, 349 F.Supp. 827 (S.D. Tex. 1972), *affirmed*, 493, F.2d 408 (5th Cir. 1974)

In April 1969 Dr. Denton Cooley implanted an artificial heart into the chest of Haskel Karp, who survived approximately 64 hours on the device and died about one day after it was replaced by a human donor heart. Mrs. Karp later brought suit, alleging among other things failure to obtain informed consent. It was established at trial that Mr. Karp had signed two consent forms. The first was the hospital's general consent form:

> I hereby authorize the physician or physicians in charge of Haskel Karp to administer any treatment; or to administer any treatment; or to administer such anesthetics and perform such operation as may be deemed necessary or advisable in the diagnosis and treatment of this patient.

Prior to surgery, Mr. Karp also signed an express consent to the implant:

> I, Haskell Karp, request and authorize Dr. Denton Cooley and such other surgeons as he may designate, to perform upon me, in St. Luke's Hospital of Houston, Texas, cardiac surgery for advanced cardiac decompensation and myocardial insufficiency as a result of numerous coronary occlusions. The risk of the surgery has been explained to me. In the event cardiac function cannot be restored by excision of destroyed heart muscle and plastic reconstruction of the ventricle and death seems to be imminent, I authorize Dr. Cooley and his staff to remove my diseased heart and insert a mechanical cardiac substitute. I understand that his mechanical device will not be permanent and ultimately will require replacement by a heart transplant. I realize that this device has been tested in the laboratory but has not been used to sustain a human being and that no assurance of success can be made. I expect the surgeons to exercise every effort to preserve my life through any of these means . . . .

Mrs. Karp's first allegation, that she did not understand how experimental the procedure was, was rejected as irrelevant. Under Texas law, only Mr. Karp had the power to consent and only his understanding was relevant. To her second allegation, her husband did not read the form before he signed it, the court said that he was legally bound by his signature on the document. The third allegation, that he was not given sufficient information, was rejected on the basis that the court found the procedure therapeutic rather than experimental. In the words of the Appeals Court: "the record contains no evidence that Mr. Karp's treatment was other than therapeutic and we agree that in this context an action for experimentation must be measured by traditional malpractice evidentiary standards."

c.  _Strunk v. Strunk_, 445 S.W.2d 145 (Ky. 1969)

The Kentucky Supreme Court upheld the donation by
a mentally retarded adult of a kidney to his brother on the
basis of court approval and consent of his mother.  The court
said:  "The right to act for the incompetent in all cases has
been recognized in this country under the doctrine of substituted judgment and is broad enough not only to cover property
but also to cover all matters touching on the well being of the
ward."  The court laid emphasis on its finding that the donation would be a "benefit" to the retarded donor since his
brother had agreed to continue to visit him after the transplant
operation.

d.  _Nathan v. Farinelli_, 74-87, Equity, Mass. Supreme
    Judicial Court (1974, Quirico, J.)

This case involved a proposed bone marrow transplant from a 6-year-old to her 10-year-old brother, who was
suffering from aplastic anemia and for whom there was an 85%
probability of death without the transplant.  After reviewing
the case law, the judge rejected the notion that the donation
could be characterized as "beneficial" for the 6-year-old, but
authorized it nonetheless on the basis that the parental decision to permit the transplant seemed "fair and reasonable"
under the circumstances:

It is unrealistic to expect or require that the
parents, finding themselves in their present difficult and try-
ing dilemma, can objectively act as they believe William and
Toni would act if they were now adults facing the same situation.  It would be more truthful to recognize that the parents
themselves are making the decisions for their children.  The
parents have the right and responsibility to make these decisions but the safeguard of judicial review is necessary because of the potential temptations resulting from the built-in
conflict of their position . . . .
What remains to be determined, therefore, is whether
the parents' decision to allow Toni to participate as a donor
in the proposed transplant operation is fair and reasonable in
the particular circumstances of this case.  To make this determination the court must weigh and balance the individual
interests of the two children.  On the one hand the court must
consider the nature and urgency of William's physical condition,
his need for the transplant, the probable benefit to him from
the transplant, the probable risks or consequences to him if the
transplantation is withheld, and the availability and efficacy
of alternative methods of treatment for his condition; and on
the other hand it must consider Toni's physical condition, the
nature and extent of her physical participation in the transplant, and the probable and possible risks and consequences to
her by reason of her participation . . . .  [I]t is the court's
conclusion that in the circumstances of this case the parents'
decision to allow Toni's participation as donor to William is
one which they have authority to make, that it is fair and reasonable as to Toni, and that it is in all respects lawful and
effective to authorize the doctors and the hospital to perform
the proposed procedure on her.

### 3. Federal Regulations

#### a.  45 Code of Federal Regulations 46.116-117

The Department of Health and Human Services promul-

gated on January 26, 1981, general requirements for informed

consent covering all research funded by the Department and all

research done at institutions operating under a general assur-

ance wherein the institution agrees to review all research pro-

jects by its Institutional Review Board (IRB).

§ 46.116  General requirements for informed consent.

Except was provided elsewhere in this or other subparts,
no investigator may involve a human being as a subject in research covered by these regulations unless the investigator has
obtained the legally effective informed consent of the subject
or the subject's legally authorized representative.  An investigator shall seek such consent only under circumstances that provide the prospective subject or the representative sufficient
opportunity to consider whether or not to participate and that
minimize the possibility of coercion or undue influence.  The
information that is given to the subject or the representative
shall be in language understandable to the subject or the representative.  No informed consent, whether oral or written, may
include any exculpatory language through which the subject or
the representative is made to waive or appear to waive any of
the subject's legal rights, or releases or appears to release
the investigator, the sponsor, the institution or its agents
from liability for negligence.
   (a) Basic elements of informed consent.  Except as provided in paragraph (c) of this section, in seeking informed
consent the following information shall be provided to each
subject:
   (1) A statement that the study involves research, an
explanation of the purposes of the research and the expected
duration of the subject's participation, a description of the
procedures to be followed, and identification of any procedures
which are experimental;
   (2) A description of any reasonably foreseeable risks
or discomforts to the subject;
   (3) A description of any benefits to the subject or to
others which may reasonably be expected from the research;
   (4) A disclosure of appropriate alternative procedures
or courses of treatment, if any, that might be advantageous to
the subject;
   (5) A statement describing the extent, if any, to which
confidentiality of records identifying the subject will be maintained;
   (6) For research involving more than minimal risk, an
explanation as to whether any compensation and an explanation
as to whether any medical treatments are available if injury
occurs and, if so, what they consist of, or where further information may be obtained;
   (7) An explanation of whom to contact for answers to
pertinent questions about the research and research subjects'
rights, and whom to contact in the event of a research-related
injury to the subject; and

(8) A statement that participation is voluntary, refusal to participate will involve no penalty or loss of benefits to which the subject is otherwise entitled, and the subject may discontinue participation at any time without penalty
or loss of benefits to which the subject is otherwise entitled.

(b) Additional elements of informed consent. When appropriate, one or more of the following elements of information
shall also be provided to each subject:

(1) A statement that the particular treatment or procedure may involve risks to the subject (or to the embryo or
fetus, if the subject is or may become pregnant) which are currently unforeseeable;

(2) Anticipated circumstances under which the subject's
participation may be terminated by the investigator without regard to the subject's consent;

(3) Any additional costs to the subject that may result from participation in the research;

(4) The consequences of a subject's decision to withdraw from the research and procedures for orderly termination
of participation by the subject;

(5) A statement that significant new findings developed during the course of the research which may relate to the
subject's willingness to continue participation will be provided to the subject; and

(6) The approximate number of subjects involved in the
study.

(c) An IRB may approve a consent procedure which does not
include, or which alters, some or all of the elements of informed consent set forth above, or waive the requirement to
obtain informed consent provided the IRB finds and documents
that:

(1) The research is to be conducted for the purpose of
demonstrating or evaluating: (i) Federal, state, or local benefit or service programs, (ii) procedures for obtaining benefits
or services under these programs, or (iii) possible changes in
or alternatives to these programs or procedures; and

(2) The research could not practicably be carried out
without the waiver or alteration.

(d) An IRB may approve a consent procedure which does not
include, or which alters, some or all of the elements of informed consent set forth above, or waive the requirements to
obtain informed consent provided the IRB finds and documents
that:

(1) The research involves no more than minimal risk
to the subjects;

(2) The waiver or alteration will not adversely affect
the rights and welfare of the subjects;

(3) The research could not practicable be carried out without the waiver or alteration; and

(4) Whenever appropriate, the subjects will be provided with additional pertinent information after participation.

(e) The informed consent requirements in these regulations are not intended to preempt any applicable federal, state, or local laws which require additional information to be disclosed in order to informed consent to be legally effective.

(f) Nothing in these regulations is intended to limit the authority of a physician to provide emergency medical care, to the extent the physician is permitted to do so under applicable federal, state, or local law.

## § 46.117  Documentation of informed consent

(a) Except as provided in paragraph (c) of this section, informed consent shall be documented by the use of a written consent form approved by the IRB and signed by the subject or the subject's legally authorized representative.  A copy shall be given to the person signing the form.

(b) Except as provided in paragraph (c) of this section, the consent form may be either of the following:

(1) A written consent document that embodies the elements of informed consent required by §46.116.  This form may be read to the subject or the subject's legally authorized representative, but in any event, the investigator shall give either the subject or the representative adequate opportunity to read it before it is signed; or

(2) A "short form" written consent document stating that the elements of informed consent required by §46.116 have been presented orally to the subject or the subject's legally authorized representative.  When this method is used, there shall be a witness to the oral presentation.  Also, the IRB shall approve a written summary of what is to be said to the subject or the representative.  Only the short form itself is to be signed by the subject or the representative.  However, the witness shall sign both the short form and a copy of the summary.  A copy of the summary shall be given to the subject or the representative, in addition to a copy of the "short form."

(c) An IRB may waive the requirement for the investigator to obtain a signed consent form of some or all subjects if it finds either:

(1) That the only record linking the subject and the research would be the consent document and the principal risk would be potential harm resulting from a breach of confidentiality.  Each subject will be asked whether the subject wants documentation linking the subject with the research, and the subject's wishes will govern; or

(2) That the research presents no more than minimal
risk of harm to subjects and involves no procedures for which
written consent is normally required outside of the research
context.

In cases where the documentation requirement is wavied, the
IRB may require the investigator to provide subjects with a
written statement regarding the research.

b.   Regulations of the Food and Drug Administration

Consent regulations promulgated by the Food and Drug

Administration for drug experimentation are identical to those

of the Department of Health and Human Services codified in 45

C.F.R. 46.116-117, with the exception of a paragraph (20 C.F.R.

50.25(5)) that specifies that the Administration may inspect

the records of such experimentation.

## A.  Eugenics and Genetic Screening


### 1.  Judicial Decisions


#### a.  *Curlender v. Bio-Science Laboratories*, 165 Cal. Rptr. 477 (Ct. App. 1980)

Plaintiff Shauna Tamar Curlender, a child, by her father, Hyam Curlender, as guardian ad litem, sought damages for personal injury from defendants Bio-Science Laboratories, a corporation, Automated Laboratory Sciences [the correct name of which is Automated Laboratory Services], a corporation, and Jerome Schaffer, M.D. . . . [D]efendants demurred to the first amended complaint in its entirety on the ground that it had failed to state a cause of action. . . . The trial court sustained the demurrers . . . leave to amend and an order of dismissal was filed.  Plaintiff has appealed from this order of dismissal.

The appeal presents an issue of first impression in California:  What remedy, if any, is available in this state to a severely impaired child--genetically defective--born as the result of defendants' negligence in conducting certain genetic tests of the child's parents--tests which, if properly done, would have disclosed the high probability that the actual, catastrophic result would occur?

In resolving this important and complex issue, we turn first to the allegations of the amended complaint, one less than artfully drawn considering the far-reaching implications--both legal and medical--of the matter.  Because of the procedural posture by which this case reaches us, we bear in mind that we must accept as true the factual allegations contained in that pleading. . . .

. . . [P]laintiff Shauna alleged that on January 15, 1977, her parents, Phillis and Hyam Curlender, retained defendant laboratories to administer certain tests designed to reveal whether either of the parents were carriers of genes which would result

135

in the conception and birth of a child with Tay-Sachs disease,
medically defined as "amaurotic familial idiocy." The tests on
plaintiff's parents were performed on January 21, 1977, and, it
was alleged, due to defendants' negligence, "incorrect and inaccurate" information was disseminated to plaintiff's parents concerning their status as carriers.

The complaint did not allege the date of plaintiff's birth,
so we do not know whether the parents relied upon the test results in conceiving plaintiff, or, as parents-to-be when the
tests were made, relied upon the results in failing to avail
themselves of amniocentesis, and an abortion. In any event, on
May 10, 1978, plaintiff's parents were informed that plaintiff
had Tay-Sachs disease.

As the result of the disease, plaintiff Shauna suffers from
"mental retardation, susceptibility to other diseases, convul-
sions, sluggishness, apathy, failure to fix objects with her
eyes, inability to take an interest in her surroundings, loss of
motor reactions, inability to sit up or hold her head up, loss
of weight, muscle atrophy, blindness, pseudobulper palsy, inability to feed orally, decerebrate rigidity and gross physical deformity." It was alleged that Shauna's life expectancy is estimated to be four years. The complaint also contained allegations
that plaintiff suffers "pain, physical and emotional distress,
fear, anxiety, despair, loss of enjoyment of life, and frustra-
tion. . . ."

The complaint sought costs of plaintiff's care as damages and
also damages for emotional distress and the deprivation of "72.6
years of her life." In addition, punitive damages of three mil-
lion dollars were sought, on the ground that "[a]t the time that
Defendants . . . [tested the parents] Defendants, and each of
them, had been expressly informed by the nation's leading authority on Tay-Sachs disease that said test procedures were substantially inaccurate and would likely result in disasterous [sic]
and catastrophic consequences to the patients, and Defendants
knew that said procedures were improper, inadequate and with in-
sufficient controls and that the results of such testing were
likely to be inaccurate and that a false negative result would
have disasterous [sic] and catastrophic consequences to the Plaintiff, all in conscious disregard of the health, safety and well-
being of Plaintiff. . . ."

. . . [T]he term "wrongful life" will be confined to those
causes of action *brought by the infant* alleging that, due to the
negligence of the defendant, birth occurred; this would include
the healthy baby boy involved in *Stills, supra,* as well as the
genetically and severely impaired plaintiff, Shauna, in the case
at bench. . . .

The term "wrongful life" appeared in 1963 in an Illinois appellate court opinion. (*Zepeda v. Zepeda* (1963) 41 Ill.App.2d
240, 190 N.E.2d 849. . . .) There the court denied recovery to

an infant plaintiff who claimed that his defendant father had injured him by causing him to be born illegitimately. The Illinois
court . . . declared that "[r]ecognition of the plaintiff's claim
means creation of a new tort:  a cause of action for *wrongful
life*. The legal implications of such a tort are vast, the social
impact could be staggering. . . ."

A major (and much cited) opinion considering a claim for damages by an impaired infant plaintiff and his parents is *Gleitman
v. Cosgrove* (1967) 49 N.J. 22, 227 A.2d 689, from the New Jersey
Supreme Court.  The Gleitmans brought a malpractice action a-
gainst Mrs. Gleitman's physician for damages because the Gleitman
child, Jeffrey, had been born with serious impairments of sight,
speech, and hearing.  Mrs. Gleitman had contracted rubella (mea-
les) during the first trimester of pregnancy (the first three
months).  Defendant was made aware of this fact, but failed to
inform the mother-to-be of any potentially harmful consequences
to her child; Mrs. Gleitman was assured by him that such consequences would not occur, although it was common medical knowledge
that rubella, contracted during early pregnancy, often causes
the type of defects suffered by Jeffrey, who was also mentally
retarded.

The majority of the *Gleitman* court barred recovery by *either*
the parents or the child on two grounds:  (1) the perceived impossibility of computing damages and (2) public policy.  With respect to the computation of damages, the court explained that
"[t]he normal measure of damages in tort actions is compensatory.
Damages are measured by comparing the conditions plaintiff would
have been in, had the defendants not been negligent, with the
plaintiff's impaired condition as a result of the negligence.
The infant plaintiff would have us measure the difference between
his life with defects against the utter void of nonexistence,
but it is impossible to make such a determination.  This Court
cannot weigh the value of life with impairements against the nonexistence of life itself.  By asserting that he should not have
been born, the infant plaintiff makes it logically impossible
for a court to measure his alleged damages because of the impossibility of making the comparison required by compensatory remedies."

Any decision negating the value of life directly or by impli-
cation was seen by the majority in *Gleitman* as an impermissible
expression of public policy. . . .

A vastly different view was expressed by a dissenting opinion in *Gleitman*.  It was there declared that the majority "permits a wrong with serious consequential injury to go wholly un-
redressed.  That provides no deterrent to professional irrespon-
sibility and is neither just nor compatible with expanding principles of liability in the field of torts. . . ."

Of some significance with respect to this question is the
fact that in 1973, *Roe v. Wade*, 410 U.S. 113, was decided by the

United States Supreme Court.  The nation's high court determined
that parents have a *constitutionally protected right* to obtain
an abortion during the first trimester of pregnancy, free of
state interference.  We deem this decision to be of considerable
importance in defining the parameters of "wrongful-life" litigation.

The *Roe v. Wade* case played a rather substantial part in the
partial retreat from the *Gleitman* holding by the New Jersey Supreme Court majority in *Berman v. Allan* (1979) 80 N.J. 421, 404
A.2d 8.  The Bermans, parents and child, brought suit for medical malpractice.  Mrs. Berman had become pregnant in her late
thirties, a circumstance involving a substantial risk that the
child would be born with Down's syndrome (mongolism), one of
the major characteristics of which is mental retardation.  Sharon Berman, the child, was so afflicted.  Amniocentesis--by that
time a well established technique for discerning birth defects
*in utero*--had not been suggested to the Bermans.  The majority
in the *Berman* court held that the *parents* had stated a cause of
action, and that they could recover damages for emotional distress, but that lifetime support for Sharon could not be awarded.

But the *Berman* court rejected the concept that the infant
Sharon possessed an independent cause of action.  Referring to
the difficulty of measuring damages in such a case, the court
declared that "[n]onetheless, were the *measure* of damages our
sole concern, it is possible that some judicial remedy could be
fashioned which would redress plaintiff, if only in part, for injuries suffered."  Here, the majority chose to rely on public
policy considerations.  The *Berman* court considered that Sharon
had not suffered any damage cognizable at law by being brought
into existence.  It was explained that "[o]ne of the most deeply
held beliefs of our society is that life--whether experienced
with or without a major physical handicap--is more precious than
non-life. . . .  Sharon, by virtue of her birth, will be able to
love and be loved and to experience happiness and pleasure--emo-
tions which are truly the essence of life and which are far more
valuable than the suffering she may endure.  To rule otherwise
would require us to disavow the basic assumption upon which our
society is based.  This we cannot do. . . ."

The dissenting opinion in *Berman* expressed the cogent observation that, as for the child, "[a]n adequate comprehension of
the infant's claims under these circumstances *starts with the re-
alization that the infant has come into this world and is here,*
encumbered by an injury attributable to the malpractice of the
doctors. . . ."

In *Park v. Chessin* (1977) 60 A.D. 80, 400 N.Y.S.2d 110, an
intermediate New York appellate court considered the following
facts.  The Parks had one child born with polycystic kidney disease, a fatal hereditary ailment.  The baby died.  The parents
consulted defendant doctors and informed them of this; assured

that the condition would not reoccur, the Parks had a second
child, who also had the disease but survived for a short life
span of 2 and ½ years.  The court held that these facts gave
both the parents and child causes of action, that "decisional
law must keep pace with expanding technological, economic and
social change.  Inherent in the abolition of the statutory ban on
abortion . . . is a public policy consideration which gives potential parents the right, within certain statutory and case law
limitations, *not* to have a child.  This right extends to instances in which it can be determined with reasonable medical
certainty that the child would be born deformed.  *The breach of
this right may also be said to be tortious to the fundamental
right of a child to be born as a whole, functional human being.*"
But this view of the law also had a short life span.  This
decision was reviewed in *Becker v. Schwartz* (1978), 46 N.Y.2d
401, 413 N.Y.S.2d 895, 386 N.E.2d 807 (as a companion case) and
overruled.  The Beckers and their mongoloid infant sought damages from medical doctors who had not, depsite the mother's age
when she became pregnant, warned of the danger or informed the
Beckers of amniocentesis.  The parents, declared *Becker*, had stated a cause of action and could recover their pecumiary loss but
*not* damages for emotional distress, as the latter recovery
would offend public policy.  The infant plaintiffs in both
*Becker* and *Park* were held to be barred from recovery because of
the inability of the law to make a comparison between human existence with handicaps and no life at all.  The court particularly rejected the idea that a child may expect life without deformity:  "There is no precedent for recognition at the Appellate Division of 'the fundamental right of a child to be born as
a whole, functional human being.' . . ."
Two decisions of note have involved Tay-Sachs impairment--
the condition involved in the case before us.  In *Howard v.
Lecher* (1977) 397 N.Y.S.2d 363, 366 N.E.2d 64, an intermediate
appellate court in New York considered an action brought by the
parents to recover damages for emotional distress from the consulting physicians.  In *Howard*, the child died.  Denying recovery, the *Howard* majority reasoned that recognition of the parents' cause of action "would require the extension of traditional tort concepts beyond manageable bounds. . . ."
In *Gildiner v. Thomas Jefferson Univ. Hospital* (E.D.Pa.1978)
451 F.Supp. 692, the parents had been tested for Tay-Sachs; the
tests indicated that amniocentesis should be performed; it was
performed, but negligently; the parents were both carriers, and
the infant born to them suffered from Tay-Sachs.  Relying on
*Gleitman v. Cosgrove, supra,* the federal district court held
that the parents could recover damages, but the child could not.
A strong public policy was perceived in allowing parental recovery:  "Tay-Sachs disease can be prevented only by accurate genetic testing combined with the right of parents to abort afflicted

fetuses within appropriate time limitations. *Society has an interest in insuring that genetic testing is properly performed and interpreted."* . . .

*First.* For clear analysis it is important to recognize certain distinctions among the cases purportedly dealing with the "wrongful-life" concept. One such distinction is that concerning the condition of the child involved. Surely there is a world of difference between an unwanted healthy child who is illegitimate, the unwanted tenth child of a marriage, and the severly deformed infant plaintiff, Shauna, in the case at bench. Illegitimacy is a status which may or may not prove to be a hindrance to one so born, depending on a multitude of other facts; it cannot be disputed that in present society such a circumstance, both socially and legally, no longer need present an overwhelming obstacle. The same is true for the simply unwanted child. We agree with the reasoning of *Zepeda* and *Stills* that a cause of action based upon impairment of status--illegitimacy contrasted with legitmacy --should not be recognizable at law *because* a necessary element for the establishment of any cause of action in tort is missing, *injury* and damages consequential to that injury. A child born with severe impairment, however, presents an entirely different situation because the necessary element of *injury* is present.

*Second.* The decisional law of other jurisdictions, while not dispositive of Shauna's claim pursuant to California law, is of considerable significance in defining the basic issues underlying the true "wrongful-life" action--one brought by the infant whose painful existence is a direct and proximate result of negligence by others. That decisional law demonstrates some measure of progression in our law. Confronted with the fact that the births of these infants may be directly traced to the negligent conduct of tohers, and that the result of that negligence is palpable injury, involving not only pecuniary loss but untold anguish on the part of all concerned, the courts in our sister states have progressed from a stance of barring all recovery to a recognition that, at least, the parents of such a child may state a cause of action founded on negligence.

We note that there has been a gradual retreat from the position of accepting "impossibility of measuring damages" as the sole ground for barring the infant's right of recovery, although the courts continue to express divergent views on how the parents' damages should be measured, in terms of allowing recovery for both pecuniary loss and damages for emotional distress, or, in recognizing one element of recovery only, but not the other.

The concept of public policy has played an important role in this developing field of law. Public policy, as perceived by most courts, has been utilized as the basis for denying recovery; in some fashion, a deeply held belief in the sanctity of life has compelled some courts to deny recovery to those among us who have been born with serious impairment.  But the dissents, written along the way, demonstrate that there is not universal acceptance of the notion that "metaphysics" or "religious beliefs," rather than law, should govern the situation; the dissents have emphasized that considerations of public policy should include regard for social welfare as affected by careful genetic counseling and medical procedures.

We have alluded to the monumental implications of *Roe v. Wade*, one of which is the present legality of, and availability of, eugenic abortion in the proper case.  Another factor of substantial proportions in "wrongful-life" litigation is the dramatic increase, in the last few decades, of the medical knowledge and skill needed to avoid genetic disaster.  As the author of the article in the Yale Law Journal points out, "Genetic defects represent an increasingly large part of the overall national health care burden."  The writer concluded that the law indeed has an appropriate function in encouraging adequate and careful medical practice in the field of genetic counseling, observing that "[t]ort law, a well-recognized means of regulating the practice of medicine, can be used both to establish and to limit the duty of physicians to fulfill this [genetic counseling] function."

*Third.*  Despite the cool reception accorded such "wrongful-life" litigation, both parents and their children have continued to seek redress for the wrongs committed, presumably for a number of reasons: (1) the serious nature of the wrong; (2) increasing sophistication as to the causes, which may not with present knowledge be attributed to the fine hand of providence but rather to lack of care; and (3) the understanding that the law reflects, perhaps later than sooner, basic changes in the way society views such matters. . . .

[W]e assess the cause of action of Shauna, the defectively born plaintiff.  We have no difficulty in ascertaining and finding the existence of a duty owed by medical laboratories engaged in genetic testing to parents and their as yet unborn children to use ordinary care in administration of available tests for the purpose of providing information concerning potential genetic defects in the unborn.  The public policy considerations with respect to the individuals involved and to society as a whole dictate recognition of such a duty, and it is of signigicance that in no decision that has come to our attention which has dealth with the "wrongful-life" concept has it been suggested that public policy considerations negate the existence of such a duty. . . .

The real crux of the problem is whether the breach of duty was the proximate cause of *an injury cognizable at law*.  The injury, of course, is not the particular defect with which a plaintiff is afflicted--considered in the abstract--but it is the birth of plaintiff with such defect.

The circumstance that the birth and injury have come hand in
hand has caused other courts to deal with the problem by barring
recovery. The reality of the "wrongful-life" concept is that
such a plaintiff both *exists* and *suffers* due to the negligence
of others. It is neither necessary nor just to retreat into medi-
tation on the mysteries of life. We need not be concerned with
the fact that had defendants not been negligent, the plaintiff
might not have come into existence at all. The certainty of genetic impairment is no longer a mystery. In addition, a reverent
appreciation of life compels recognition that plaintiff, however
impaired as she may be, has come into existence as a living person with certain rights.

One of the fears expressed in the decisional law is that,
once it is determined that such infants have rights cognizable
at law, nothing would prevent such plaintiff from bringing suit
against its own parents for allowing plaintiff to be born. In
our view, the fear is groundless. The "wrongful-life" cause of
action with which we are concerned is based upon negligently
caused failure by someone under a duty to do so to inform the
prospective parents of facts needed by them to make a conscious
choice *not* to become parents. If a case arose where, despite
due care by the medical profession in transmittting the necessary warnings, parents made a conscious choice to proceed with a
pregnancy, with full knowledge that a seriously impaired infant
would be born, that conscious choice would provide an intervening act of proximate cause to preclude liability insofar as defendants other than the parents were concerned. Under such circumstances, we see no sound public policy which should protect
those parents from being answerable for the pain, suffering and
misery which they have wrought upon their offspring. . . .

[W]e have long adhered to the principle that there should be
a remedy for every wrong committed. "Fundamental in our jurisprudence is the principle that for every wrong there is a remedy
and that an injured party should be compensated for all damage
proximately caused by the wrongdoer. . . ."

We have concluded that it is clearly consistent with the applicable principles of the statutory and decisional tort law in
this state to recognize a cause of action stated by plaintiff a-
gainst the defendants. . . .

The extent of recovery, however, is subject to certain limitations due to the nature of the tort involved. While ordinarily
a defendant is liable for all consequences flowing from the injury, it is appropriate in the case before us to tailor the elements of recovery, taking into account particular circumstances
involved.

The complaint seeks damages based upon an actuarial life expectancy of more than 70 years--the life expectancy if plaintiff
had been born without the Tay-Sachs disease. The complaint sets
forth that plaintiff's actual life expectancy, because of the dis-

ease, is only four years.  We reject as untenable the claim that
plaintiff is entitled to damages as if plaintiff had been born
without defects and would have had a normal life expectancy.
Plaintiff's right to damages must be considered on the basis of
plaintiff's mental and physical condition at birth and her expected condition during the short life span (four years according
to the complaint) anticipated for one with her impaired condition.  In similar fashion, we reject the notion that a "wrongful-
life" cause of action involves any attempted evaluation of a
claimed right *not* to be born.  In essence, we construe the
"wrongful-life" cause of action by the defective child as the
right of such child to recover damages for the pain and suffering to be endured during the limited life span available to such
a child and any special pecuniary loss resulting from the impaired condition. . . .
  [W]e find that plaintiff has adequately pleaded a cause of
action for punitive damages.  We see no reason in public policy
or legal analysis for exempting from liability for punitivie damages a defendant who is sued for committing a "wrongful-life"
tort.


  b.  *Buck v. Bell*, 274 U.S. 200 (1927)

Carrie Buck, "the daughter of a feeble-minded mother and the

mother of an illegitimate feeble-minded child," brought suit a-

gainst the Superintendent of the State Colony for Epileptics and

the Feeble Minded on the grounds that the sterilization which

was performed on her at his instigation was unlawful because

the statute authorizing it, after an in-hospital review, violated

her rights under the Fourteenth Amendment.  The lower court de-

nied her petition, and the U.S. Supreme Court affirmed, with Jus-

tice Oliver Wendell Holmes writing the majority opinion, a por-

tion of which reads as follows:

  . . . There can be no doubt that so far as procedure is concerned the rights of the patient are most carefully considered,
and as every step in this case was taken in scrupulous compliance
with the statute and after months of observation, there is no
doubt that in that respect the plaintiff in error has had due

process at law.

The attack is not upon the procedure but upon the substantive law. It seems to be contended that in no circumstances could such an order be justified. It certainly is contended that the order cannot be justified upon the existing grounds. The judgment finds the facts that have been recited and that Carrie Buck "is the probable potential parent of socially inadequate offspring, likewise afflicted, that she may be sexually sterilized without detriment to her general health and that her welfare and that of society will be promoted by her sterilization," and thereupon makes the order. In view of the general declarations of the Legislature and the specific findings of the Court obviously we cannot say as matter of law that the grounds do not exist, and if they exist they justify the result. We have seen more than once that the public welfare may call upon the best citizens for their lives. It would be strange if it could not call upon those who already sap the strength of the State for these lesser sacrifices, often not felt to be such by those concerned, in order to prevent our being swamped with incompetence. It is better for all the world, if instead of waiting to execute degenerate offspring for crime, or to let them starve for their imbecility, society can prevent those who are manifestly unfit from continuing their kind. The principle that sustains compulsory vaccination is broad enough to cover cutting the Fallopian tubes. *Jacobson v. Massachusetts*, 197 U.S. 11. Three generations of imbeciles are enough.

But, it is said, however it might be if this reasoning were applied generally, it fails when it is confined to the small number who are in the institutions named and is not applied to the multitudes outside. It is the usual last resort of constitutional arguments to point out shortcomings of this sort. But the answer is that the law does all that is needed, when it does all that it can, indicates a policy, applies it to all within the lines, and seeks to bring within the lines all similarly situated so far and so fast as its means allow. Of course so far as the operations enable those who otherwise must be kept confined to be returned to the world, and thus open the asylum to others, the equality aimed at will be more nearly reached.

c.   *In the Matter of Lee Ann Grady*, 426 A.2d 467 (N.J. 1981)

Lee Ann Grady, a 19-year-old with Down's Syndrome, was the

oldest of three children, lived at home with her parents, and

had never been institutionalized. Her I.Q. is in the "upper 20s

to upper 30s range," and she can converse, dress, and bathe herself.  Her parents have provided her with birth control pills for
the past four years, but now that she will leave her special
class and enter a sheltered workshop her parents wish to have her
sterilized to prevent conception because they do not believe she
is capable of understanding pregnancy nor of caring for a baby on
her own.  The hospital refused to perform the sterilization without court authorization.

The lower court granted the parents' application; the Appeals
Court approves routine court review of such decisions (under the
*parens patriae* power).  In this regard it distinguished the
*Grady* decision from the *Quinlan* decision, where routine judicial
review was not required because the decision in *Quinlan* seemed
"more clear cut," indefinite life in a coma versus natural death,
and had to be made more on the basis of instinct than logic.
Having set the court up as the decision-maker, the next issue was
to define the criteria a court must use in arriving at the decision.  The court determined that its role was to determine the in-
compentent's *best interests*, considering the following factors:

1. the possibility of pregnancy;

2. the possibility of physical and mental harm from pregnancy
   and sterilization;

3. the likelihood of sexual activity;

4. the inability of the person to understand contraception;

5. the feasibility of a less drastic means of contraception;

(continued on page 148)

# SURVEY OF NEWBORN SCREENING PROGRAMS

The status of screening programs in the United States is dynamic and is constantly in the process of change. This report is a reflection of the information available to NCHGD as of July 31, 1980. For the most current information on screening programs for a particular state, please contact the Maternal and Child Health Director for that state.

| | Phenylketonuria (PKU) | Hypothyroidism | Homocystinuria | Maple Syrup Urine Disease | Galactosemia | Tyrosinemia | Sickle Cell Anemia | Other | Metabolic Screening Advisory Committee |
|---|---|---|---|---|---|---|---|---|---|
| Alaska | ● | ● | ● | ● | ● | ● | | | |
| Alabama | ● | ● | | | | | | | |
| Arizona | ● | ● | ● | ● | ● | | ● | | ● |
| Arkansas | ● | v | | | | | | | |
| California * | ● | ● | | | ● | | ●[1] | | ●[2] |
| Colorado | ● | ● | ● | ● | ● | | ● | | |
| Connecticut | ● | ● | | | ● | | | | |
| Delaware | v | v | v | v | v | v | | | |
| District of Columbia* | ● | ● | | | | | | | ● |
| Florida | ● | ● | | ● | ● | | | | ● |
| Georgia | ● | ● | ● | ● | ● | ● | ● | | |
| Hawaii | ● | | | | | | | | |
| Idaho | ● | ● | ● | ● | ● | ● | | | |
| Illinois | ● | ● | | | | | ●[1] | | |
| Indiana | ● | ● | | | | | | | ● |
| Iowa * | ● | v | | v | v | | | | |
| Kansas | ● | ● | | | | | ●[1] | | |
| Kentucy | ● | ● | | | ● | | | | |
| Louisiana | ● | ● | | | | | ● | | |
| Maine | ● | ● | ● | ● | ● | | | | |
| Maryland | ● | ● | ● | ● | ● | | ●[1] | | ●[3] |
| Massachusetts | ● | ● | ● | ● | ● | | ●[1] | ●[4] | |
| Michigan | ● | v | | | | | | | ●[5] |
| Minnesota | ● | ● | | | ● | | | | |
| Mississippi | ● | ● | | | | | | | |
| Missouri | ● | ● | | | | | ●[1] | | |

See footnotes at end of table

| | Phenylketonuria (PKU) | Hypothyroidism | Homocystinuria | Maple Syrup Urine Disease | Galactosemia | Tyrosinemia | Sickle Cell Anemia | Other | Metabolic Screening Advisory Committee |
|---|---|---|---|---|---|---|---|---|---|
| Montana | ● | ● | ● | ● | ● | ● | | | |
| Nebraska | ● | ● | | | | | | | |
| Nevada | ● | ● | ● | ● | ● | ● | | | |
| New Hampshire | ● | v | | | | | | | |
| New Jersey | ● | ● | | | | | ●[1] | | |
| New Mexico | ● | ● | ● | ● | ● | | ● | | |
| New York | ● | ● | ● | ● | ● | | ●[1] | ●[6] | ●[7] |
| North Carolina | v | | | | v | v | ● | | |
| North Dakota | ● | ● | | | | | | | |
| Ohio | ● | ● | ● | | ● | | ●[1] | | |
| Oklahoma | ● | ● | | | | | | | |
| Oregon | ● | ● | ● | ● | ● | ● | | | |
| Pennsylvania | ● | ● | | | | | | | ● |
| Rhode Island | ● | v | v | v | v | | | | |
| South Carolina | ● | ● | | | | | | | |
| South Dakota | ● | | | | | | | | |
| Tennessee | ● | ● | | | | | | | |
| Texas | ● | ● | ● | | ● | | | | |
| Utah | ● | ● | | | ● | | | | |
| Vermont | v | v | | | v | | | | ● |
| Virginia | ● | ● | | | | | ●[1] | | |
| Washington | ● | ● | | | | | | | |
| West Virginia | ● | ● | | | | | | | |
| Wisconsin | ● | ● | | ● | ● | | | | ● |
| Wyoming | ● | ● | ● | ● | ● | | ● | | ● |

v = voluntary, no statutory authority

* effective October 1980

1 on request
2 California genetic disease unit
3 Maryland Commission on Hereditary Disorders

4 tuberous sclerosis effective in 1986
5 Chronic Diseases Advisory Committee
6 histidinemia/adenosine deaminase deficiency
7 New York Birth Defects Institute

6. the possibility of postponing sterilization;

7. ability of the person to care for a child, or the possibility
   of marriage at a future date with ability of the couple to
   care for the child;

8. evidence of relevant medical advances; and

9. demonstration that the proponents of sterilization are seeking
   it in good faith for the primary concern of the person and not
   for their own or the public's convenience.

In short, the court found a new substantive right--the right
to sterilization--and sought to protect incompetents from its ar-
bitrary use by demanding strict due process protections prior to
sterilization authorization.

B.  Recombinant DNA Research

1.  Brief Chronology of Key Events

1973-1974   Publications on use of restriction enzymes for form-
            ing recombinant DNA molecules.

1973        At Gordon Research Conference on Nucleic Acids, con-
            cerns are voiced about possible biohazards of "hybrid
            molecules."  Singer and Soll write to President of
            National Academy of Sciences; copy of letter is pub-
            lished in *Science* (v. 191, p. 1114).  NAS forms com-
            mittee, chaired by Paul Berg.

1973        Berg discusses his plans for SV-40-*E.coli* recombinant
            DNA experiments with Jim Watson and others; does not
            conduct the research because of concerns about bio-
            hazards.

July 1974   Berg's NAS Committee on Recombinant DNA issues state-
            ment that, based on "potential rather than demonstra-
            ted risk," (1) calls for an international voluntary
            moratorium on 2 types of experiments, (2) requests
            National Institutes of Health (NIH) to form an Advi-
            sory Committee to oversee experiments, develop safety
            procedures, and devise research guidelines, and (3)
            suggests international meeting to review research and
            discuss ways of dealing with potential biohazards.

March 1975  International meeting recommended by Berg's Committee
            meets at Asilomar, California.  Conferees discuss *po-
            tential* risks and benefits of recombinant DNA re-
            search and legal and public policy questions, debate
            controlling scientific research vs. allowing autono-
            my, and issue a six-part report.  The report began by
            affirming the "revolutionary" impact of recombinant
            DNA methodology and ended by proposing physical and
            biological containment procedures that would allow
            work to "proceed with appropriate safeguards."

May 1975    N.Y. Academy of Sciences and Institute of Society,
            Ethics and the Life Sciences hold conference on "Eth-
            ical and Scientific Issues Posed by Human Uses of Mo-
            lecular Genetics."

Aug.-Sept.  Erwin Chargoff criticizes the "molecular bishops and
1975        church fathers" who gathered at Asilomar for what he
            felt was a self-protective, societally irresponsible

report.

July 1975    First draft of NIH Committee Guidelines (Hognes Sub-
             committee) is issued; it is revised and weakened by
             8 of 12 members of subcommittee at Woods Hole meet-
             ing.  Woods Hole draft sets up P1 to P4 physical con-
             tainment and EK1 to EK3 biological containment levels
             for experiments.  Draft is criticized as too lax by
             Barg and 49 other petition signers, and by Genetics
             and Society group (Jonathan King et al.) of Scien-
             tists and Engineers for Social and Political Action
             (SESPA).  Criticism also directed at composition of
             NIH Committee for not encompassing a range of scien-
             tific disciplines and public representation.  In re-
             sponse to criticisms of Woods Hole Draft, NIH Commit-
             tee's head (DeWitt Stetter) appoints second subcom-
             mittee (Kutter group) to propose alternative guide-
             lines.

Dec. 1975    NIH Committee meets for 2 days to draft guidelines.
             Debate centers around how tc classify experiments on
             P1-P4 and EK1-EK3 scales and how to classify certain
             types of "shotgun experiments."  Newly developed
             methods to construct "disarmed" (biologically "safe")
             *E. coli* help committee draft tighter guidelines than
             Woods Hole version.

Apr. 1975    Senate Health Subcommittee holds hearings on public
             policy for recombinant DNA.

Feb. 1976    Fredrickson (Director, NIH) holds hearings on pro-
             posed guidelines.  First major forum for non-scien-
             tist input.  Critics contend that guidelines not
             strict enough in containment requirements and ques-
             tion how any NIH guidelines would be generally en-
             forceable.

June 1976    Final NIH hearings on guidelines.  Debates take
             place at institutions such as Harvard about construc-
             tion of containment facilities, with increasing com-
             munity concern and involvement (e.g., hearings by
             Cambridge City Council).

Jan. 1977    Cambridge Experimentation Committee submits final Re-
             port to the City Council favoring research with fur-
             ther restrictions.

Mar.-Apr.    California State legislature holds hearings on a pro-
1977         posed statute to control DNA research.

June 1977    Senator Edward Kennedy introduces legislation to con-
             trol DNA research on the federal level.

July 1977    Scientists begin to argue that risks are almost non-
             existent and that therefore no outside controls or
             monitoring of the research is necessary; i.e., they
             claim they made a mistake in suggesting public par-
             ticipation in the first place.

Dec. 1978    Revised federal guidelines appear in 43 *Federal Reg-
             ister* 60080 (Dec. 22, 1978), including the following
             passages in the introduction:

             > "The final guidelines relax some of the restric-
             > tions under which recombinant DNA research has
             > been conducted since 1976, and at the same time
             > increase the role of the public in monitoring re-
             > combinant DNA experiments."

             > "The revisions exempt altogether five categories
             > of experiments from the guidelines' restric-
             > tions."

             > "The revised guidelines will ease restrictions
             > on other permissible experiments."

Nov. 1980    Further revisions in federal guidelines appear in 45
             *Federal Register* 77384 (Nov. 21, 1980):  "The pur-
             pose of these Guidelines is to specify practices for
             constructing and handling (i) recombinant DNA mole-
             cules and (ii) organisms and viruses containing re-
             combinant DNA molecules."

July 1981    The most recent federal guidelines are presented in
             46 *Federal Register* 34462 (July 1, 1981).

Nov. 1981    A Notice to Proposed Actions under NIH Guidelines
             for Research Involving Recombinant DNA Molecules,
             passed by a 16-5 vote of the Recombinant DNA Adviso-
             ry Committee (RAC), is published in 46 *Federal Reg-
             ister* 59734 (Dec. 7, 1981).  This action superseded
             a previous RAC proposal (46 *FR* 59368, Dec. 4, 1981).
             The proposal of December 7 upholds the compulsory
             status of the guidelines, yet relaxes some of the
             regulations governing federally funded recombinant
             DNA research, such as those on containment.  Insti-
             tutionalized biosafety committees are retained in
             this proposal, as are prohibitions on three types of
             experiments requiring approval by a local biosafety
             group, as well as NIH and the RAC.

May 1982    Further revisions in federal guidelines proposed;
            47 *Federal Register* (May 26, 1982).

2. <u>Guidelines of the National Institutes of Health and the
   Department of Health, Education, and Welfare, published
   in 41 *Federal Register* 27911 (June 23, 1976)</u>

## I.  INTRODUCTION

The purpose of these guidelines is to recommend safeguards
for research on recombinant DNA molecules to the National Institutes of Health and to other institutions that support such research.  In this context we define recombinant DNAs as molecules
that consist of different segments of DNA which have been joined
together in cell-free systems, and which have the capacity to in-
fect and replicate in some host cell, either autonomously or as
an integrated part of the host's genome.
    This is the first attempt to provide a detailed set of guide-
lines for use by study sections as well as practicing scientists
for evaluating research on recombinant DNA molecules.  We cannot
hope to anticipate all possible lines of imaginative research
that are possible with this powerful new methodology.  Nevertheless, a considerable volume of written and verbal contributions
from scientists in a variety of disciplines has been received.
In many instances the views presented to us were contradictory.
At present, the hazards may be guessed at, speculated about, or
voted upon, but they cannot be known absolutely in the absence
of firm experimental data--and, unfortunately, the needed data
were, more often than not, unavailable.  Our problem then has
been to construct guidelines that allow the promise of the methodology to be realized while advocating the considerable caution
that is demanded by what we and others view as potential hazards.
    In designing these guidelines we have adopted the following
principles, which are consistent with the general conclusions
that were formulated at the International Conference on Recombinant DNA Molecules held at Asilomar Conference Center, Pacific
Grove, California, in February 1975:  (i) There are certain experiments for which the assessed potential hazard is so serious
that they are not to be attempted at the present time.  (ii)  The
remainder can be undertaken at the present time provided that the
experiment is justifiable on the basis that new knowledge or benefits to humankind will accrue that cannot readily be obtained by
use of conventional methodology and that appropriate safeguards
are incorporated into the design and execution of the experiment.
In addition to an insistence on the practice of good microbiological techniques, these safeguards consist of providing both physical and biological barriers to the dissemination of the poten-

tially hazardous agents. (iii) The level of containment provided by these barriers is to match the estimated potential hazard for each of the different classes of recombinants. For projects in a given class, this level is to be highest at initiation
and modified subsequently only if there is a substantiated change
in the assessed risk or in the applied methodology. (iv) The
guidelines will be subjected to periodic review (at least annual-
ly) and modified to reflect improvements in our knowledge of the
potential biohazards and of the available safeguards.

In constructing these guidelines it has been necessary to define boundary conditions for the different levels of physical and
biological containment and for the classes of experiments to
which they apply. We recognize that these definitions do not
take into account existing and anticipated special procedures and
information that will allow particular experiments to be carried
out under different conditions than indicated here without sacri-
fice of safety. Indeed, we urge that individual investigators
devise simple and more effective containment procedures and that
study sections give consideration to such procedures which may
allow change in the containment levels recommended here.

It is recommended that all publications dealing with recombinant DNA work include a description of the physical and biological containment procedures practiced, to aid and forewarn others
who might consider repeating the work.

## II. CONTAINMENT

Effective biological safety programs have been operative in
a variety of laboratories for many years. Considerable information therefore already exists for the design of physical containment facilities and the selection of laboratory procedures applicable to organisms carrying recombinant DNAs. The existing programs rely upon mechanisms that, for convenience, can be divided
into two categories: (i) a set of standard practices that are
generally used in microbiological laboratories, and (ii) special
procedures, equipment, and laboratory installations that provide
physical barriers which are applied in varying degrees according
to the estimated biohazard.

Experiments on recombinant DNAs by their very nature lend
themselves to a third containment mechanism--namely, the application of highly specific biological barriers. In fact, natural
barriers do exist which either limit the infectivity of a vector
or vehicle (plasmid, bacteriophage or virus) to specific hosts,
or its dessemination and survival in the environment. The vectors that provide the means for replication of the recombinant
DNAs and/or the host cells in which they replicate can be genetically designed to decrease by many orders of magnitude the probability of dissemination of recombinant DNAs outside the laboratory.

As these three means of containment are complementary, different levels of containment appropriate for experiments with different recombinants can be established by applying different combinations of the physical and biological barriers to a constant use of the standard practices. We consider these categories of containment separately here in order that such combinations can be conveniently expressed in the guidelines for research on the different kinds of recombinant DNA (Section III).

A. *Standard practices and training.* The first principle of containment is a strict adherence to good microbiological practices. Consequently, all personnel directly or indirectly involved in experiments on recombinant DNAs must receive adequate instruction. This should include at least training in aseptic techniques and instruction in the biology of the organisms used in the experiments so that the potential biohazards can be understood and appreciated.

Any research group working with agents with a known or potential biohazard should have an emergency plan which describes the procedures to be followed if an accident contaminates personnel or environment. The principal investigator must ensure that everyone in the laboratory is familiar with both the potential hazards of the work and the emergency plan. If a research group is working with a known pathogen for which an effective vaccine is available, all workers should be immunized. Serological monitoring, where appropriate, should be provided.

B. *Physical containment levels.* A variety of combinations (levels) of special practices, equipment, and laboratory installations that provide additional physical barriers can be formed. For example, 31 combinations are listed in "Laboratory Safety at the Center for Disease Control"; four levels are associated with the "Classification of Etiologic Agents on the Basis of Hazard"; four levels were recommended in the "Summary Statement on the Asilomar Conference on Recombinant DNA Molecules"; and the National Cancer Institute uses three levels for research on oncogenic viruses. We emphasize that these are an aid to, and not a substitute for, good technique. Personnel must be competent in the effective use of all equipment needed for the required containment level as described below. We define only four levels of physical containment here, both because the accuracy with which one can presently assess the biohazards that may result from recombinant DNAs does not warrant a more detailed classification, and because additional flexibility can be obtained by combination of the physical with the biological barriers. Though different in detail, these four levels ($P1 < P2 < P3 < P4$) approximate those given for human etiologic agents by the Center for Disease Control (i.e., classes 1 through 4), in the Asilomar summary statement (i.e., minimal, low, moderate, and high), and by the National Cancer Institute for oncogenic viruses (i.e., low, moderate, and high), as is indicated by the P-number or adjective in the following headings.  It should be emphasized that the descriptions and assignments of physical containment detailed below are based on existing approaches to containment of hazardous organisms.

We anticipate, and indeed already know of, procedures which enhance physical containment capability in novel ways.  For example, miniaturization of screening, handling, and analytical procedures provides substantial containment of a given host-vector system.  Thus, such procedures should reduce the need for the standard types of physical containment, and such innovations will be considered by the Recombinant DNA Molecule Program Advisory Committee.

The special practices, equipment and facility installations indicated for each level of physical containment are required for the safety of laboratory workers, other persons, and for the protection of the environment.  Optional items have been excluded; only those items deemed absolutely necessary for safety are presented.  Thus, the listed requirements present basic safety criteria for each level of physical containment.  Other microbiological practices and laboratory techniques which promote safety are to be encouraged.  Additional information giving further guidance on physical containment is provided in a supplement to the guidelines.

*P1 Level (Minimal).*  A laboratory suitable for experiments involving recombinant DNA molecules requiring physcial containment at the P1 level is a laboratory that possesses no special engineering design features.  It is a laboratory commonly used for microorganisms of no or minimal biohazard under ordinary conditions of handling.  Work in this laboratory is generally conducted on open bench tops.  Special containment equipment is neither required nor generally available in this laboratory.  The laboratory is not separated from the general traffic patterns of the building.  Public access is permitted.

The control of biohazards at the P1 level is provided by standard microbiological practices of which the following are examples:  (i)  Laboratory doors should be kept closed while experiments are in progress.  (ii)  Work surfaces should be decontaminated daily and following spills of recombinant DNA materials.  (iii)  Liquid wastes containing recombinant DNA materials should be decontaminated before disposal.  (iv)  Solid wastes contaminated with recombinant DNA materials should be decontaminated or packaged in a durable leak-proof container before removal from the laboratory.  (v)  Although pipetting by mouth is permitted, it is preferable that mechanical pipetting devices be used.  When pipetting by mouth, cotton-plugged pipettes shall be employed.  (vi)  Eating, drinking, smoking, and storage of food in the working area should be discouraged.  (vii)  Facilities to wash hands should be available.  (viii)  An insect and rodent control program should be provided.  (ix)  The use of laboratory gowns is discretionary with the laboratory supervisor.

   *P2 Level (Low).* A laboratory suitable for experiments involving recombinant DNA molecules requiring physical containment
at the P2 level is similar in construction and design to the P1
laboratory. The P2 laboratory must have access to an autoclave
within the building; it may have a Biological Safety Cabinet.
Work which does not produce a considerable aerosol is conducted
on the open bench. Although this laboratory is not separated
from the general traffic patterns of the building, access to the
laboratory is limited when experiments requiring P2 level physical containment are being conducted. Experiments of lesser biohazard potential can be carried out concurrently in carefully demarcated areas of the same laboratory.

   The P2 laboratory is commonly used for experiments involving
microorganisms of low biohazard such as those which have been
classified by the Center for Disease Control as Class 2 agents.

   The following practices shall apply to all experiments requiring P2 level physical containment: (i) Laboratory doors
shall be kept closed while experiments are in progress. (ii)
Only persons who have been advised of the potential biohazard
shall enter the laboratory. (iii) Children under 12 years of
age shall not enter the laboratory. (iv) Work surfaces shall
be decontaminated daily and immediately following spills of recombinant DNA materials. (v) Liquid wastes of recombinant DNA
materials shall be decontaminated or packaged in a durable leak-
proof container before removal from the laboratory. Packaged materials shall be disposed of by incineration or sterilized before disposal by other methods. Contaminated materials that are
to be processed and reused (i.e., glassware) shall be decontaminated before removal from the laboratory. (vii) Pipetting by
mouth is prohibited; mechanical pipetting devices shall be used.
(viii) Eating, drinking, smoking, and storage of food are not
permitted in the working area. (ix) Facilities to wash hands
shall be available within the laboratory. Persons handling recombinant DNA materials should be encouraged to wash their hands
frequently and when they leave the laboratory. (x) An insect
and rodent control program shall be provided. (xi) The use of
laboratory gowns, coats, or uniforms is required. Such clothing
shall not be worn to the lunch room or outside the building.
(xii) Animals not related to the experiment shall not be permitted in the laboratory. (xiii) Biological Safety Cabinets
and/or other physical containment equipment shall be used to minimize the hazard of aerosolization of recombinant DNA materials
from operations or devices that produce a considerable aerosol
(e.g., blender, lyophilizer, sonicator, shaking machine, etc.).
(xiv) Use of the hypodermic needle and syringe shall be avoided
when alternate methods are available.

   *P3 Level (Moderate).* A laboratory suitable for experiments
involving recombinant DNA molecules requiring physical contain-

ment at the P3 level has special engineering design features and
physical containment equipment.  The laboratory is separated
from areas which are open to the general public.  Separation is
generally achieved by controlled access corridors, air locks,
locker rooms, or other double-doored facilities which are not a-
vailable for use by the general public.  Access to the laboratory
is controlled.  Biological Safey Cabinets are available within
the controlled laboratory area.  The surfaces of walls, floors,
bench tops, and ceilings are easily cleanable to facilitate housekeeping and space decontamination.
    Directional air flow is provided within the controlled labora-
tory area.  The ventilation system is balanced to provide for an
inflow of supply air from the access corridor into the laboratory.  The general exhaust air from the laboratory is discharged
outdoors and so dispersed to the atmosphere to prevent reentry
into the building.  No recirculation of the exhaust air shall be
permitted without appropriate treatment.
    No work in open vessels involving hosts or vectors contain-
ing recombinant DNA molecules requiring P3 physical containment
is conducted on the open bench.  All such procedures are confined
to the Biological Safety Cabinets.
    The following practices shall apply to all experiments re-
quiring P3 level physical containment:  (i)  The universal biohazard sign is required on all laboratory access doors.  Only
persons whose entry into the laboratory is required on the basis
of program or support needs shall be authorized to enter.  Such
persons shall be advised of the potential biohazards before entry and they shall comply with posted entry and exit procedures.
Children under 12 years of age shall not enter the laboratory.
(ii)  Laboratory doors shall be kept closed while experiments are
in progress.  (iii)  Biological Safety Cabinets and other physical containment equipment shall be used for all procedures that
produce aerosols of recombinant DNA materials (e.g., pipetting,
plating, flaming, transfer operations, grinding, blending, dry-
ing, sonicating, shaking, etc.).  (iv)  The work surfaces of Biological Safety Cabinets and other equipment shall be decontaminated following the completion of the experimental activity contained within them.  (v)  Liquid wastes containing recombinant
DNA materials shall be decontaminated before disposal.  (vi)  Solid wastes contaminated with recombinant DNA materials shall be decontaminated or packaged in a durable, leak-proof container before removal from the laboratory.  Packaged material shall be
sterilized before disposal.  Contaminated materials that are to
be processed and reused (i.e., glassware) shall be sterilized in
the controlled laboratory area or placed in a durable leak-proof
container before removal from the controlled laboratory area.
This container shall be sterilized before the materials are processed.  (vii)  Pipetting by mouth is prohibited; mechanical pi-

petting devices shall be used. (viii) Eating, drinking, smoking, and storage of food are not permitted in the laboratory. (ix) Facilities to wash hands shall be available within the laboratory. Persons shall wash hands after experiments involving recombinant DNA materials and before leaving the laboratory. (x) An insect and rodent control program shall be provided. (xi) Laboratory clothing that protects street clothing (i.e., long sleeve solid-front or wrap-around gowns, no-button or slipover jackets, etc.) shall be worn in the laboratory. FRONT-BUTTON LABORATORY COATS ARE UNSUITABLE. Gloves shall be worn when handling recombinant DNA materials. Provision for laboratory shoes is recommended. Laboratory clothing shall not be worn outside the laboratory and shall be decontaminated before it is sent to the laundry. (xii) Raincoats, overcoats, topcoats, coats, hats, caps, and such street outerwear shall not be kept in the laboratory. (xiii) Animals and plants not related to the experiment shall not be permitted in the laboratory. (xiv) Vacuum lines shall be protected by filters and liquid traps. (xv) Use of the hypodermic needle and syringe shall be avoided when alternate methods are available. (xvi) If experiments of lesser biohazard potential are to be conducted in the same laboratory concurrently with experiments requiring P3 level physical containment they shall be conducted only in accordance with all P3 level requirements. (xvii) Experiments requiring P3 level physical containment can be conducted in laboratories where the directional air flow and general exhaust air conditions described above cannot be achieved, provided that this work is conducted in accordance with all other requirements listed and is contained in a Biological Safety Cabinet with attached glove ports and gloves. All materials before removal from the Biological Safety Cabinet shall be sterilized or transferred to a non-breakable, sealed container, which is then removed from the cabinet through a chemical decontamination tank, autoclave, ultraviolet air lock, or after the entire cabinet has been decontaminated.

   *P4 Level (High).* Experiments involving recombinant DNA molecules requiring physical containment at the P4 level shall be confined to work areas in a facility of the type designed to contain microorganisms that are extremely hazardous to man or may cause serious epidemic disease. The facility is either a separate building or it is a controlled area, within a building, which is completely isolated from all other areas of the building. Access to the facility is under strict control. A specific facility operations manual is available. Class III Biological Safety Cabinets are available within work areas of the facility.

   A P4 facility has engineering features which are designed to prevent the escape of microorganisms to the environment. These features include: (i) Monolithic walls, floods, and ceilings in which all penetrations such as for air ducts, electrical conduits, and utility pipes are sealed to assure the physical isolation of the work area and to facilitate housekeeping and space decontamination; (ii) air locks through which supplies and materials can be brought safely into the facility; (iii) contiguous clothing change and shower rooms through which personnel enter into and exit from the facility; (iv) double-door autoclaves to sterilize and safely remove wastes and other materials from the facility; (v) a biowaste treatment system to sterilize liquid effluents if facility drains are installed; (vi) a separate ventilation system which maintains negative air pressures and directional air flow within the facility; and (vii) a treatment system to decontaminate exhaust air before it is dispersed to the atmosphere. A central vacuum utility system is not encouraged; if one is installed, each branch line leading to a laboratory shall be protected by a high efficiency particulate air filter.

The following practices shall apply to all experiments requiring P4 level physical containment: (i) the universal biohazard sign is required on all facility access doors and all interior doors to individual laboratory rooms where experiments are conducted. Only persons whose entry into the facility or individual laboratory rooms is required on the basis of program or support needs shall be authorized to enter. Such persons shall be advised of the potential biohazards and instructed as to the appropriate safeguards to ensure their safety before entry. Such persons shall comply with the instructions and all other posted entry and exit procedures. Under no condition shall children under 15 years of age be allowed entry. (ii) Personnel shall enter into and exit from the facility only through the clothing change and shower rooms. Personnel shall shower at each exit from the facility. The air locks shall not be used for personnel entry or exit except for emergencies. (iii) Street clothing shall be removed in the outer facility side of the clothing change area and kept there. Complete laboratory clothings including undergarments, pants and shirts or jumpsuits, shoes, head cover, and gloves shall be provided and used by all persons who enter into the facility. Upon exit, this clothing shall be stored in lockers provided for this purpose or discarded into collection hampers before personnel enter into the shower area. (iv) Supplies and materials to be taken into the facility shall be placed in an entry air lock. After the outer door (opening to the corridor outside of facility) has been secured, personnel occupying the facility shall retrieve the supplies and materials by opening the interior air lock door. This door shall be secured after supplies and materials are brought into the facility. (v) Doors to laboratory rooms within the facility shall be kept closed while experiments are in progress. (vi) Experimental procedures requiring P4 level physical containment shall be confined to Class III Biological Safety Cabinets. All materials, before removal from these cabinets, shall be sterilized or transferred to a non-breakable sealed container, which is then removed from the system through a chemical decontaminated tank, autoclave, or after the entire system has been decontaminated.

(vii) No materials shall be removed from the facility unless they have been sterilized or decontaminated in a manner to prevent the release of agents requiring P4 physical containment. All wastes and other materials and equipment not damaged by high temperature or steam shall be sterilized in the double-door autoclave. Biological materials to be removed from the facility shall be transferred to a non-breakable sealed container which is then removed from the facility through a chamber designed for gas sterilization. Other materials which may be damaged by temperature or steam shall be sterilized by gaseous or vapor methods in an air lock or chamber designed for this purpose. (viii) Eating, drinking, smoking, and storage of food are not permitted in the facility. Foot-operated water fountains located in the facility corridors are permitted. Separate potable water piping shall be provided for these water fountains. (ix) Facilities to wash hands shall be available within the facility. Persons shall wash hands after experiments. (x) An insect and rodent control program shall be provided. (xi) Animals and plants not related to the experiment shall not be permitted in the facility. (xii) If a central vacuum system is provided, each vaccum outlet shall be protected by a filter and liquid trap in addition to the branch line HEPA filter mentioned above. (xiii) Use of the hypodermic needle and syringe shall be avoided when alternate methods are available. (xiv) If experiments of lesser biohazard potential are to be conducted in the facility concurrently with experiments requiring P4 level containment, they shall be confined in Class I or Class II Biological Safey Cabinets or isolated by other physical containment equipment. Work surfaces of Biological Safety Cabinets and other equipment shall be decontaminated following the completion of the experimental activity contained within them. Mechanical pipetting devices shall be used. All other practices listed above with the exception of (vi) shall apply.

C. *Shipment.* To protect product, personnel, and the environment, all recombinant DNA material will be shipped in containers that meet the requirements issued by the U.S. Public Health Service, Department of Transportation, and the Civil Aeronautics Board for shipment of etiologic agents.

D. *Biological containment levels.* Biological barriers are specific to each host-vector system. Hence the criteria for this mechanism of containment cannot be generalized to the same extent as for physical containment. This is particularly true at the present time when our experience with existing host-vector systems and our predictive knowledge about projected systems are sparse. The classification of experiments with recombinant DNAs that is necessary for the construction of the experimental guide-

lines (Section III) can be accomplished with least confusion if
we use the host-vector system as the primary element and the
source of the inserted DNA as the secondary element in the classification.  It is therefore convenient to specify the nature of
the biological containment under host-vector headings such as
those given below for *Escherichia coli* K-12.

## III.   EXPERIMENTAL GUIDELINES

A general rule that, though obvious, deserves statement is
that the level of containment required for any experiment on DNA
recombinants shall never be less than that required for the most
hazardous component used to construct and clone the recombinant
DNA (i.e., vector, host, and inserted DNA).  In most cases the
level of containment will be greater, particularly when the recombinant DNA is formed from species that ordinarily do not ex-
change genetic information.  Handling the purified DNA will generally require less stringent precautions than will propagating
the DNA.  However, the DNA itself should be handled at least as
carefully as one would handle the most dangerous of the DNAs
used to make it.

The above rule by itself effectively precludes certain exper-
iments--namely, those in which one of the components is in Class
5 of the "Classification of Etiologic Agents on the Basis of Hazard," as these are excluded from the United States by law and
USDA administrative policy.  There are additional experiments
which may engender such serious biohazards that they are not to
be performed at this time.  These are considered prior to presentation of the containment guidelines for permissible experiments.

A.  *Experiments that are not to be performed.*  We recognize
that it can be argued that certain of the recombinants placed in
this category could be adequately contained at this time.  Nonetheless, our estimates of the possible dangers that may ensue if
that containment fails are of such a magnitude that we consider
it the wisest policy to at least defer experiments on these recombinant DNAs until there is more information to accurately assess that danger and to allow the construction of more effective
biological barriers.  In this respect, these guidelines are more
stringent than those initially recommended.

The following experiments are not to be initiated at the
present time:  (i) Cloning of recombinant DNAs derived from the
pathogenic organisms in Classes 3, 4, and 5 of "Classification
of Etiologic Agents on the Basis of Hazard," or oncogenic viruses classified by NCI as moderate risk, or cells known to be
infected with such agents, regardless of the host-vector system
used.  (ii) Deliberate formation of recombinant DNAs containing
genes for the biosynthesis of potent toxins (e.g., botulinum or
diphtheria toxins; venoms from insects, snakes, etc.).  (iii)
Deliberate creation from plant pathogens of recombinant DNAs

that are likely to increase virulence and host range.  (iv) Deliberate release into the environment of any organism containing
a recombinant DNA molecule.  (v) Transfer of a drug resistance
trait to microorganisms that are not known to acquire it natural-
ly if such acquisition could compromise the use of a drug to control disease agents in human or veterinary medicine or agricul-
ture.

In addition, at this time large-scale experiments (e.g.,
more than 10 liters of culture) with recombinant DNAs known to
make harmful products are not to be carried out.  We differenti-
ate between small- and large-scale experiments with such DNAs because the probability of escape from containment barriers normally increases with increasing scale.  However, specific experiments in this category that are of direct social benefit may be
excepted from this rule if special biological containment precautions are used, and provided that these experiments are expressly approved by the Recombinant DNA Molecule Program Advisory Committee of NIH.

B.  *Containment guidelines for permissible experiments.*  It
is anticipated that most recombinant DNA experiments initiated
before these guidelines are next reviewed (i.e., within the
year) will employ *E. coli* K-12 host-vector systems.  These are
also the systems for which we have the most experience and knowledge regarding the effectiveness of the containment provided by
existing hosts and vectors necessary for the construction of
more effective biological barriers.

For these reasons, *E. coli* K-12 appears to be the system of
choice at this time, although we have carefully considered arguments that many of the potential dangers are compounded by using
an organism as intimately connected with man as is *E. coli*.
Thus, while proceeding cautiously with *E. coli*, serious efforts
should be made toward developing alternate host-vector systems;
this subject is discussed in considerable detail in Appendix A.

We therefore consider DNA recombinants in *E. coli* before
proceeding to other host-vector systems. . . .

On May 26, 1982, revisions to the guidelines were proposed

in 47 *Federal Register* 23110.  Most proposed changes were proce-

dural.  However, the membership of an Institution Biosafety Com-

mittee (IBC) was defined.

"IV-B-2.  *Membership and Procedures of the IBC.*  The institution shall establish an Institutional Biosafety Committee (IBC)
whose responsibilities need not be restricted to recombinant DNA.
The committee shall meet the following requirements: . . ."
    d. The requirement specifying that 20% of the IBC membership

be nonaffiliated with the Institution would be eliminated.  Section IV-D-2-a would be renumbered and modified to read as follows:

"IV-B-2-a.  The IBC shall comprise no fewer than five members so selected that they collectively have experience and expertise in recombinant DNA technology and the capability to assess the safety of recombinant DNA research experiments and any potential risk to public health or the environment.  At least two members shall not be affiliated with the Institution (apart from their membership on the IBC) and shall represent the interest of the surrounding community with respect to health and protection of the environment.  Members meet this requirement if, for example, they are officials of State or local public health or environmental protection agencies, members of other local governmental bodies, or persons active in medical, occupational health, or environmental concerns in the community.  The Biological Safety Officer (BSO), mandatory when research is being conducted at the P3 and P4 levels, shall be a member.  (See Section IV-B-4.)"

e.  The language of Section IV-D-2-b on professional competence and the specification on laboratory staff would be renumbered and modified to read as follows:

"IV-B-2-b.  In order to ensure the competence necessary to review recombinant DNA activities, it is recommended that (i) the IBC include persons with expertise in recombinant DNA technology, biological safety, and physical containment; (ii) the IBC include, or have available as consultants, persons knowledgeable in institutional commitments and policies, applicable law, standards of professional conduct and practice, community attitudes, and the environment; and (iii) at least one member be from the laboratory technical staff."


3.  Guidelines of the Cambridge (Massachusetts) Experimentation Review Board

These "Guidelines for the Use of Recombinant DNA Molecule Technology in the City of Cambridge" were submitted to the Commissioner of Health and Hospitals on December 21, 1976, and to the City Manager on January 5, 1977.

Introduction

The Cambridge Experimentation Review Board has spent nearly four months studying the controversy over the use of the recom-

binant DNA technology in the City of Cambridge. The following
charge was issued to the Board by the City Manager at the request
of the City Council on August 6, 1976.

The broad responsibility of the Experimentation Review Board
shall be to consider whether research on recombinant DNA which
is proposed to be conducted at the P3 level of containment in
Cambridge may have any adverse effect on public health within
the City, and for this purpose to undertake, among other studies,
to:

    (a) review the "Decision of the Director, National Institutes
        of Health, to Release Guidelines for Research on Recombi-
        nant DNA Molecules" dated and released on June 23, 1976;
    (b) review but not be limited to the methods of physical and
        biological containment recommended by the NIH;
    (c) review methods for monitoring compliance with applicable
        procedural safeguards;
    (d) review methods for monitoring compliance with safeguards
        applicable to physical containment;
    (e) review procedures for handling accidents (e.g., fire) in
        recombinant DNA research facilities;
    (f) advise the Commissioner of Health and Hospitals on the
        reviews, findings, and recommendations.

Throughout our inquiry we recognized that the controversy
over recombinant DNA research involves profound philosophical issues that extend beyond the scope of our charge. The social and
ethical implications of genetic research must receive the broad-
est possible dialogue in our society. That dialogue should address the issue of whether all knowledge is worth pursuing. It
should examine whether any particular route to knowledge threat-
ens to transgress upon our precious human liberties. It should
raise the issue of technology assessment in relation to long-
range hazards to our natural and social ecology. Finally, a national dialogue is needed to determine how such policy decisions
are resolved in the framework of participatory democracy. . . .

Section 1:

After reviewing the guidelines issued by the Director of the
National Institutes of Health (NIH) for Research Involving Recombinant DNA Molecules (issued June 23, 1976) it is the unanimous
judgment of the Cambridge Experimentation Review Board that Recombinant DNA research can be permitted in Cambridge provided
that:

The research is undertaken with strict adherence to the NIH
Guidelines and in addition to those guidelines the following conditions are met:

    I. Institutions proposing recombinant DNA research or pro-
       posing to use the recombinant DNA technology shall pre-
       pare a manual which contains all procedures relevant to

the conduct of said research at all levels of containment
and that training in appropriate safeguards and procedures for minimizing potential accidents should be mandatory for all laboratory personnel.

II.  The Institutional Biohazards Committee mandated by the
NIH Guidelines should be broad-based in its composition.
It should include members from a variety of disciplines,
representation from the bio-technicians staff and at
least one community representative unaffiliated with the
institution.  The community representative should be approved by the Health Policy Board of the City of Cambridge.

III.  All experiments undertaken at the P3 level of physical
containment shall require an NIH certified host-vector
system of at least an EK2 level of biological containment.

IV.  Institutions undertaking recombinant DNA experiments
shall perform adequate screening to insure the purity of
the strain of host organisms used in the experiments and
shall test organisms resulting from such experiments for
their resistance to commonly used therapeutic antibiotics.

V.  As part of the institution's health monitoring responsibilities it shall in good faith make every attempt, subject to the limitation of the available technology, to
monitor the survival and escape of the host organism or
any component thereof in the laboratory worker.  This
should include whatever means is available to monitor
the intestinal flora of the laboratory worker.

VI.  A Cambridge Biohazards Committee (CBC) be established
for the purpose of overseeing all recombinant DNA research that is conducted in the City of Cambridge.

  A.  The CBC shall be composed of the Commissioner of Public Health, the Chairman of the Health Policy Board
and a minimum of three members to be appointed by
the City Manager.

  B.  Specific responsibilities of the CBC shall include:
  1.  Maintaining a relationship with the institutional
biohazards committees.
  2.  Reviewing all proposals for recombinant DNA research to be conducted in the City of Cambridge
for compliance with the current NIH guidelines.
  3.  Developing a procedure for members of institutions where the research is carried on to report
to the CBC violations either in technique or established policy.
  4.  Reviewing reports and recommendations from local
institutional biohazards committees.
  5.  Carrying out site visits to institutional facilities.

      6.   Modifying these recommendations to relect future
          developments in federal guidelines.
      7.   Seeing that conditions designated as I-V in this
          section are adhered to.

Section 2:

We recommend that a city ordinance be passed to the effect
that any recombinant DNA molecule experiments undertaken in the
city which are not in strict adherence to the NIH guidelines as
supplemented in Section I of this report constitute a health hazard to the City of Cambridge.

Section 3:

We urge that the City Council of Cambridge, on behalf of
this Board and the citizenry of the country, make the following
recommendations to the Congress:

    I.   That all uses of recombinant DNA molecule technology
        fall under uniform federal guidelines and that legis-
        lation be enacted in Congress to insure conformity to
        such guidelines in all sectors, both profit and non-prof-
        it, whether such legislation takes a form of licensing
        or regulation, and that Congress appropriate sufficient
        funding to adequately enforce compliance with the legis-
        lation.
    II.   That the NIH or other agencies funding recombinant DNA
        research require institutions to include a health moni-
        toring program as part of their funding proposal and
        that monies be provided to carry out the monitoring.
   III.   That a federal registry be established of all workers
        participating in recombinant DNA research for the pur-
        pose of long-term epidemiological studies.
    IV.   That federal initiative be taken to sponsor and fund re-
        search to determine the survival and escape of the host
        organism in the human instestine under laboratory condi-
        tions.

This book is one of four publications intended to engage a broad range of persons in informed decision-making regarding key health and human value questions.  Each publication has a useful-ness of its own, while all four comprise a convenient series.

This handbook, <u>Biomedical-Ethical Issues: A Digest of Law and Policy Development</u>, contains excerpts and summaries of influential court decisions, state and federal legislation, and federal guide-lines, as well as policy statements from various religious and professional organizations, related to biomedical-ethical issues. By providing excerpts, the digest enables the general reader and the legal specialist to understand the recent evolution of public policy and to recognize those areas of public policy that remain incomplete and, in some cases, contradictory.

Also available in the series are:

*   <u>Health and Human Values: A Guide to Making Your Own Decisions</u>, by Frank Harron, John Burnside, M.D., and Tom Beauchamp.  The main text of the series contains case studies and background discussions of important moral, medical, and legal topics, selected readings from prominent writers in medicine, theology, philosophy, law, and related fields, and annotated bibliographies of recommended articles, books, anthologies, literary works, and audio-visual resources.

*   <u>Leader's Manual</u> for <u>Health and Human Values: A Guide to Making Your Own Decisions</u>.  For persons leading study groups, continuing professional education courses, and academic classes concentrating on biomedical-ethical issues, this manual offers suggestions for making best use of the cases and discussions in the primary study book, organizing learning activities, and selecting further references for group discussion.

*   <u>Human Values in Medicine and Health Care: Audio-Visual Resources</u>. Approximately 400 audio-visual items are listed; most are annotated, and all provide full information about purchase and rental costs and the names and addresses of distributors.  Two indexes list the items by topic and by format (film, videocassette, audio-cassette, or slide/tape).

These publications are offered to the general reader,
patients and their families, physicians, nurses, and other
health care practitioners, clergy, attorneys, educators,
students, legislators, and activists who seek to influence
public policy. It is hoped that they will be used to help
inform our thinking about the crucial health and human value
choices facing us all today.

Ordering Information

To place an order for any book in the Health and Human
Values series, write or call:

Yale University Press
Sales Department
92A Yale Station
New Haven, CT 06520

Tel.: (203) 432-4840